CIMA Exam Practice Kit

GW01260610

P2 – Performance Management

CIMA Exam Practice Kit

CIMA
PUBLISHING

P2 – Performance Management

Jo Avis

ELSEVIER

Amsterdam • Boston • Heidelberg • London • New York • Oxford
Paris • San Diego • San Francisco • Singapore • Sydney • Tokyo

CIMA Publishing
An imprint of Elsevier
Linacre House, Jordan Hill, Oxford OX2 8DP
30 Corporate Drive, Burlington, MA 01803

British Library Cataloguing in Publication Data
A catalogue record for this book is available from the British Library

Library of Congress Cataloging in Publication Data
A catalogue record for this book is available from the Library of Congress

978-1-85617-742-9

For information on all CIMA Publishing Publications
visit our website at www.cimapublishing.com

Typeset by Macmillan Publishing Solutions
(www.macmillansolutions.com)

Printed and bound in Great Britain

09 10 11   11 10 9 8 7 6 5 4 3 2 1

Working together to grow
libraries in developing countries

www.elsevier.com | www.bookaid.org | www.sabre.org

ELSEVIER   BOOK AID
            International   Sabre Foundation

Contents

Syllabus Guidance, Learning Objectives and Verbs

A The syllabus

The syllabus for the CIMA Professional Chartered Management Accounting qualification 2005 comprises three learning pillars:

- Management Accounting pillar
- Business Management pillar
- Financial Management pillar.

Within each learning pillar there are three syllabus subjects. Two of these subjects are set at the lower "Managerial" level, with the third subject positioned at the higher "Strategic" level. All subject examinations have a duration of three hours and the pass mark is 50%.

Note: In addition to these nine examinations, students are required to gain three years relevant practical experience and successfully sit the Test of Professional Competence in Management Accounting (TOPCIMA).

B Aims of the syllabus

The aims of the syllabus are:

- To provide for the Institute, together with the practical experience requirements, an adequate basis for assuring society that those admitted to membership are competent to act as management accountants for entities, whether in manufacturing, commercial or service organisations, in the public or private sectors of the economy.
- To enable the Institute to examine whether prospective members have an adequate knowledge, understanding and mastery of the stated body of knowledge and skills.
- To complement the Institute's practical experience and skills development requirements.

C Study weightings

A percentage weighting is shown against each topic in the syllabus. This is intended as a guide to the proportion of study time each topic requires.

All topics in the syllabus must be studied, since any single examination question may examine more than one topic, or carry a higher proportion of marks than the percentage study time suggested.

The weightings *do not* specify the number of marks that will be allocated to topics in the examination.

D Learning outcomes

Each topic within the syllabus contains a list of learning outcomes, which should be read in conjunction with the knowledge content for the syllabus. A learning outcome has two main purposes:

1 to define the skill or ability that a well-prepared candidate should be able to exhibit in the examination;
2 to demonstrate the approach likely to be taken by examiners in examination questions.

The learning outcomes are part of a hierarchy of learning objectives. The verbs used at the beginning of each learning outcome relate to a specific learning objective, for example, evaluate alternative approaches to budgeting.

The verb "evaluate" indicates a high-level learning objective. As learning objectives are hierarchical, it is expected that at this level, students will have knowledge of different budgeting systems and methodologies and be able to apply them.

A list of the learning objectives and the verbs that appear in the syllabus learning outcomes and examinations, follows:

Learning objective	Verbs used	Definition
1 Knowledge *What you are expected to know*	List	Make a list of
	State	Express, fully or clearly, the details of/facts of
	Define	Give the exact meaning of
2 Comprehension *What you are expected to understand*	Describe	Communicate the key features of
	Distinguish	Highlight the differences between
	Explain	Make clear or intelligible/State the meaning of
	Identify	Recognise, establish or select after consideration
	Illustrate	Use an example to describe or explain something

3 **Application**

How you are expected to apply
your knowledge

Apply	To put to practical use
Calculate/ compute	To ascertain or reckon mathematically
Demonstrate	To prove with certainty or to exhibit by practical means
Prepare	To make or get ready for use
Reconcile	To make or prove consistent/ compatible
Solve	Find an answer to
Tabulate	Arrange in a table

4 **Analysis**

How you are expected to
analyse the detail of what you
have learned

Analyse	Examine in detail the structure of
Categorise	Place into a defined class or division
Compare and contrast	Show the similarities and/or differences between
Construct	To build up or compile
Discuss	To examine in detail by argument
Interpret	To translate into intelligible or familiar terms
Produce	To create or bring into existence

5 **Evaluation**

How you are expected to use
your learning to evaluate,
make decisions or
recommendations

Advise	To counsel, inform or notify
Evaluate	To appraise or assess the value of
Recommend	To advise on a course of action

Learning Outcomes, Syllabus Content and Examination Format

Paper P2 – Performance Management

Syllabus Overview

While Paper P2 continues the analytic theme of Paper P1 Performance Operations (for example in terms of identifying relevant costs), its main focus is on the application of information in the management processes of decision-making and control, so as to optimise performance. The first two sections deal respectively with the key contributors to operational performance – revenue (decisions of what to produce, at what price) and costs (how to manage them to maximise profitability). The role of control in monitoring and improving performance then comes to the fore in the final two sections, dealing with principles and practices in the use of responsibility centres and budgeting.

Syllabus Structure

The syllabus comprises the following topics and study weightings:

A	Pricing and Product Decisions	30%
B	Cost Planning and Analysis for Competitive Advantage	30%
C	Budgeting and Management Control	20%
D	Control and Performance Measurement of Responsibility Centres	20%

Assessment Strategy

There will be a written examination paper of 3 hours, plus 20 minutes of pre-examination question paper reading time. The examination paper will have the following sections:

Section A – 50 marks
Five compulsory medium answer questions, each worth 10 marks. Short scenarios may be given, to which some or all questions relate.

Section B – 50 marks
One or two compulsory questions. Short scenarios may be given, to which questions relate.

Learning Outcomes and Indicative Syllabus Content

P2 – A. Pricing and Product Decisions (30%)

Learning Outcomes		Indicative Syllabus Content
Lead	**Component**	
1. Discuss concepts of cost and revenue relevant to pricing and product decisions. (4)	(a) Discuss the principles of decision-making including the identification of relevant cash flows and their use alongside non-quantifiable factors in making rounded judgements.	• Relevant cash flows and their use in short-term decisions, typically concerning acceptance/rejection of contracts, pricing and cost/benefit comparisons. (A)
	(b) Discuss the possible conflicts between cost accounting for profit reporting and stock valuation and information required for decision-making.	• The importance of strategic, intangible and non-financial judgements in decision-making. (A)
	(c) Discuss the particular issues that arise in pricing decisions and the conflict between 'marginal cost' principles and the need for full recovery of all costs incurred.	• Relevant costs and revenues in decision-making and their relation to accounting concepts. (B)
		• Marginal and full cost recovery as bases for pricing decisions in the short and long-term. (C)
2. Analyse short-term pricing and product decisions, using cost-volume-profit analysis. (4)	(a) Explain the usefulness of dividing costs into variable and fixed components in the context of short-term decision-making.	• Simple product mix analysis in situations where there are limitations on product/service demand and one other production constraint. (A, B)
	(b) Apply and interpret variable/fixed cost analysis in multiple product contexts to breakeven analysis and product mix decision-making, including circumstances where there are multiple constraints and linear programming methods are needed to identify 'optimal' solutions.	• Multi-product breakeven analysis, including breakeven and profit/volume charts, contribution/sales ratio, margin of safety, etc. (B)
	(c) Discuss the meaning of 'optimal' solutions and demonstrate how linear programming methods can be employed for profit maximising, revenue maximising and satisfying objectives.	• Linear programming for more complex situations involving multiple constraints. Solution by graphical methods of two variable problems, together with understanding of the mechanics of simplex solution, shadow prices, etc. (Note: Questions requiring the full application of the simplex algorithm will not be set although candidates should be able to formulate an initial tableau, interpret a final simplex tableau and apply the information it contained in a final tableau.) (C)
	(d) Analyse the impact of uncertainty and risk on decision models based on CVP analysis.	• Sensitivity analysis of CVP-based decision models. (D)

(continued)

Learning Outcomes

Lead	Component	Indicative Syllabus Content
3. Discuss pricing strategies and their consequences. (4)	(a) Apply an approach to pricing based on profit maximisation in imperfect markets; and discuss the financial consequences of alternative pricing strategies. (b) Discuss the financial consequences of alternative pricing strategies. (c) Explain why joint costs must be allocated to final products for financial reporting purposes, but why this is unhelpful when decisions concerning process and product viability have to be taken.	• Pricing decisions for profit maximising in imperfect markets. (Note: Tabular methods of solution are acceptable.) (A) • Pricing strategies and the financial consequences of market skimming, premium pricing, penetration pricing, loss leaders, product bundling/optional extras and product differentiation to appeal to different market segments. (B) • The allocation of joint costs and decisions concerning process and product viability based on relevant costs and revenues. (C)

P2 – B. Cost Planning and Analysis for Competitive Advantage (30%)

Learning Outcomes

Lead	Component	Indicative Syllabus Content
1. Discuss and apply evaluate techniques for analysing and managing costs for competitive advantage. (4)	(a) Compare and contrast value analysis and functional cost analysis.	• Value analysis and quality function deployment. (A)
	(b) Evaluate the impacts of just-in-time production, the theory of constraints and total quality management on efficiency, inventory and cost.	• The benefits of just-in-time production, total quality management and theory of constraints and the implications of these methods for decision-making in the 'new manufacturing environment'. (B)
	(c) Explain the concepts of continuous improvement and Kaizen costing that are central to total quality management and prepare cost of quality reports.	• Kaizen costing, continuous improvement and cost of quality reporting. (C, D)
	(d) Prepare cost of quality reports.	• Learning curves and their use in predicting product/service costs, including derivation of the learning rate and the learning index. (E)
	(e) Explain and apply learning curves to estimate time and cost for new products and services.	• Activity-based management in the analysis of overhead and its use in improving the efficiency of repetitive overhead activities. (F, G)
	(f) Apply the techniques of activity-based management in identifying cost drivers/activities; and explain how process re-engineering can be used to eliminate non-value adding activities and reduce activity costs.	• Target costing. (H)
		• Life cycle costing and implications for marketing strategies. (I)
	(g) Explain how process re-engineering can be used to eliminate non-value adding activities and reduce activity costs.	• The value chain and supply chain management, including the trend to outsource manufacturing operations to transition and developing economies. (J)
	(h) Explain how target costs can be derived from target prices and describe the relationship between target costs and standard costs.	• Gain sharing arrangements in situations where, because of the size of the project, a limited number of contractors or security issues (e.g. in defence work), normal competitive pressures do not apply. (K)
	(i) Discuss the concept of life cycle costing and how life cycle costs interact with marketing strategies at each stage of the life cycle.	• The use of direct and activity-based cost methods in tracing costs to 'cost objects', such as customers or distribution channels, and the comparison of such costs with appropriate revenues to establish 'tiered' contribution levels, as in the activity-based cost hierarchy. (L)
		• Pareto analysis. (M)

(continued)

Learning Outcomes

Lead

Component

(j) Discuss the concept of the value chain and the management of contribution/profit generated throughout the chain.

(k) Discuss gain sharing arrangements whereby contractors and customers benefit if contract targets for cost, delivery, etc. are beaten.

(l) Analyse direct customer profitability and extend this analysis to distribution channel profitability through the application of activity-based costing ideas.

(m) Apply Pareto analysis as a convenient technique for identifying key elements of data and in presenting the results of other analyses, such as activity-based profitability calculations.

Indicative Syllabus Content

P2 – C. Budgeting and Management Control (20%)

Learning Outcomes		Indicative Syllabus Content
Lead	**Component**	
1. Explain the principles that underlie the use of budgets in control. (2)	(a) Explain the concepts of feedback and feed-forward control and their application in the use of budgets for planning and control. (b) Explain the concept of responsibility accounting and its importance in the construction of functional budgets that support the overall master budget. (c) Identify controllable and uncontrollable costs in the context of responsibility accounting and explain why uncontrollable costs may or may not be allocated to responsibility centres.	• Control system concepts. (A) • The use of budgets in planning: 'rolling budgets' for adaptive planning. (A) • Responsibility accounting and the use of budgets for control: controllable costs and; treatment of uncontrollable costs; the conceptual link between standard costing and budget flexing. (B, C)
2. Evaluate performance using budgets, recognising alternative approaches and sensitivity to variable factors. (5)	(a) Evaluate projected performance using ratio analysis. (b) Calculate and evaluate the consequences of 'what if' scenarios and evaluate their impact on the master budget. (c) Evaluate performance using fixed and flexible budget reports.	• Assessing the financial consequences of projected performance through key metrics including profitability, liquidity and asset turnover ratios. (A) • What-if analysis based on alternate projections of volumes, prices and cost structures and the use of spreadsheets in facilitating these analyses. (B) • The evaluation of out-turn performance using variances based on 'fixed' and 'flexed' budgets. (C)
3. Discuss the broader managerial issues arising from the use of budgets in control. (4)	(a) Discuss the impact of budgetary control systems and setting of standard costs on human behaviour. (b) Discuss the role of non-financial performance indicators; and compare and contrast traditional approaches to budgeting with recommendations based on the 'balanced scorecard'. (c) Compare and contrast traditional approaches to budgeting with recommendations based on the 'balanced scorecard'. (d) Discuss the criticisms of budgeting, particularly from the advocates of 'beyond budgeting' techniques.	• Behavioural issues in budgeting: participation in budgeting and its possible beneficial consequences for ownership and motivation; participation in budgeting and its possible adverse consequences for 'budget padding' and manipulation; setting budget targets for motivation; implications of setting standard costs, etc. (A) • Non-financial performance indicators. (B) • Criticisms of budgeting and the recommendations of the advocates of the balanced scorecard and 'beyond budgeting'. (C, D)

Examination Techniques

Essay questions

Your essay should have a clear structure, that is, an introduction, a middle and an end. Think in terms of 1 mark for each relevant point made.

Numerical questions

It is essential to show workings in your answer. If you come up with the wrong answer and no workings, the examiner cannot award any marks. However, if you get the wrong answer but apply the correct technique then you will be given some marks.

Reports and memorandum

Where you are asked to produce an answer in a report type format you will be given easy marks for style and presentation.

- A *report* is a document from an individual or group in one organisation sent to an individual or group in another.
- A *memorandum* is an informal report going from one individual or group to another individual or group in the same organisation.

You should start a report as follows:

    To: J. SMITH, CEO, ABC plc

    From: M ACCOUNTANT

    Date: 31 December 2000

    Terms of Reference: Financial Strategy of ABC plc

Multiple choice questions managerial level

From May 2005 some multiple choice questions will be worth more than two marks. Even if you get answer wrong, you may still get some marks for technique. Therefore show all workings on such questions.

INDICATIVE MATHS TABLES AND FORMULAE

Present Value Table

Present value of £1 i.e. $(1 + r)^{-n}$ where r = interest rate; n = number of periods until payment or receipt.

Periods (n)	Interest rates (r)																			
	1%	2%	3%	4%	5%	6%	7%	8%	9%	10%	11%	12%	13%	14%	15%	16%	17%	18%	19%	20%
1	0.990	0.980	0.971	0.962	0.952	0.943	0.935	0.926	0.917	0.909	0.901	0.893	0.885	0.877	0.870	0.862	0.855	0.847	0.840	0.833
2	0.980	0.961	0.943	0.925	0.907	0.890	0.873	0.857	0.842	0.826	0.812	0.797	0.783	0.769	0.756	0.743	0.731	0.718	0.706	0.694
3	0.971	0.942	0.915	0.889	0.864	0.840	0.816	0.794	0.772	0.751	0.731	0.712	0.693	0.675	0.658	0.641	0.624	0.609	0.593	0.579
4	0.961	0.924	0.888	0.855	0.823	0.792	0.763	0.735	0.708	0.683	0.659	0.636	0.613	0.592	0.572	0.552	0.534	0.516	0.499	0.482
5	0.951	0.906	0.863	0.822	0.784	0.747	0.713	0.681	0.650	0.621	0.593	0.567	0.543	0.519	0.497	0.476	0.456	0.437	0.419	0.402
6	0.942	0.888	0.837	0.790	0.746	0.705	0.666	0.630	0.596	0.564	0.535	0.507	0.480	0.456	0.432	0.410	0.390	0.370	0.352	0.335
7	0.933	0.871	0.813	0.760	0.711	0.665	0.623	0.583	0.547	0.513	0.482	0.452	0.425	0.400	0.376	0.354	0.333	0.314	0.296	0.279
8	0.923	0.853	0.789	0.731	0.677	0.627	0.582	0.540	0.502	0.467	0.434	0.404	0.376	0.351	0.327	0.305	0.285	0.266	0.249	0.233
9	0.914	0.837	0.766	0.703	0.645	0.592	0.544	0.500	0.460	0.424	0.391	0.361	0.333	0.308	0.284	0.263	0.243	0.225	0.209	0.194
10	0.905	0.820	0.744	0.676	0.614	0.558	0.508	0.463	0.422	0.386	0.352	0.322	0.295	0.270	0.247	0.227	0.208	0.191	0.176	0.162
11	0.896	0.804	0.722	0.650	0.585	0.527	0.475	0.429	0.388	0.350	0.317	0.287	0.261	0.237	0.215	0.195	0.178	0.162	0.148	0.135
12	0.887	0.788	0.701	0.625	0.557	0.497	0.444	0.397	0.356	0.319	0.286	0.257	0.231	0.208	0.187	0.168	0.152	0.137	0.124	0.112
13	0.879	0.773	0.681	0.601	0.530	0.469	0.415	0.368	0.326	0.290	0.258	0.229	0.204	0.182	0.163	0.145	0.130	0.116	0.104	0.093
14	0.870	0.758	0.661	0.577	0.505	0.442	0.388	0.340	0.299	0.263	0.232	0.205	0.181	0.160	0.141	0.125	0.111	0.099	0.088	0.078
15	0.861	0.743	0.642	0.555	0.481	0.417	0.362	0.315	0.275	0.239	0.209	0.183	0.160	0.140	0.123	0.108	0.095	0.084	0.074	0.065
16	0.853	0.728	0.623	0.534	0.458	0.394	0.339	0.292	0.252	0.218	0.188	0.163	0.141	0.123	0.107	0.093	0.081	0.071	0.062	0.054
17	0.844	0.714	0.605	0.513	0.436	0.371	0.317	0.270	0.231	0.198	0.170	0.146	0.125	0.108	0.093	0.080	0.069	0.060	0.052	0.045
18	0.836	0.700	0.587	0.494	0.416	0.350	0.296	0.250	0.212	0.180	0.153	0.130	0.111	0.095	0.081	0.069	0.059	0.051	0.044	0.038
19	0.828	0.686	0.570	0.475	0.396	0.331	0.277	0.232	0.194	0.164	0.138	0.116	0.098	0.083	0.070	0.060	0.051	0.043	0.037	0.031
20	0.820	0.673	0.554	0.456	0.377	0.312	0.258	0.215	0.178	0.149	0.124	0.104	0.087	0.073	0.061	0.051	0.043	0.037	0.031	0.026

Cumulative Present Value of £1

This table shows the Present Value of £1 per annum. Receivable or Payable at the end of each year for n years $\dfrac{1-(1+r)^{-n}}{r}$

Periods (n)	1%	2%	3%	4%	5%	6%	7%	8%	9%	10%	11%	12%	13%	14%	15%	16%	17%	18%	19%	20%
1	0.990	0.980	0.971	0.962	0.952	0.943	0.935	0.926	0.917	0.909	0.901	0.893	0.885	0.877	0.870	0.862	0.855	0.847	0.840	0.833
2	1.970	1.942	1.913	1.886	1.859	1.833	1.808	1.783	1.759	1.736	1.713	1.690	1.668	1.647	1.626	1.605	1.585	1.566	1.547	1.528
3	2.941	2.884	2.829	2.775	2.723	2.673	2.624	2.577	2.531	2.487	2.444	2.402	2.361	2.322	2.283	2.246	2.210	2.174	2.140	2.106
4	3.902	3.808	3.717	3.630	3.546	3.463	3.387	3.312	3.240	3.170	3.102	3.037	2.974	2.914	2.855	2.798	2.743	2.690	2.639	2.589
5	4.853	4.713	4.580	4.452	4.329	4.212	4.100	3.993	3.890	3.791	3.696	3.605	3.517	3.433	3.352	3.274	3.199	3.127	3.058	2.991
6	5.795	5.601	5.417	5.242	5.076	4.917	4.767	4.623	4.486	4.355	4.231	4.111	3.998	3.889	3.784	3.685	3.589	3.498	3.410	3.326
7	6.728	6.472	6.230	6.002	5.786	5.582	5.389	5.206	5.033	4.868	4.712	4.564	4.423	4.288	4.160	4.039	3.922	3.812	3.706	3.605
8	7.652	7.325	7.020	6.733	6.463	6.210	5.971	5.747	5.535	5.335	5.146	4.968	4.799	4.639	4.487	4.344	4.207	4.078	3.954	3.837
9	8.565	8.162	7.786	7.435	7.108	6.802	6.515	6.247	5.995	5.759	5.537	5.328	5.132	4.946	4.772	4.607	4.451	4.303	4.163	4.031
10	9.471	8.983	8.530	8.111	7.722	7.360	7.024	6.710	6.418	6.145	5.889	5.650	5.426	5.216	5.019	4.833	4.659	4.494	4.339	4.192
11	10.368	9.787	9.253	8.760	8.306	7.887	7.499	7.139	6.805	6.495	6.207	5.938	5.687	5.453	5.234	5.029	4.836	4.656	4.486	4.327
12	11.255	10.575	9.954	9.385	8.863	8.384	7.943	7.536	7.161	6.814	6.492	6.194	5.918	5.660	5.421	5.197	4.988	4.793	4.611	4.439
13	12.134	11.348	10.635	9.986	9.394	8.853	8.358	7.904	7.487	7.103	6.750	6.424	6.122	5.842	5.583	5.342	5.118	4.910	4.715	4.533
14	13.004	12.106	11.296	10.563	9.899	9.295	8.745	8.244	7.786	7.367	6.982	6.628	6.302	6.002	5.724	5.468	5.229	5.008	4.802	4.611
15	13.865	12.849	11.938	11.118	10.380	9.712	9.108	8.559	8.061	7.606	7.191	6.811	6.462	6.142	5.847	5.575	5.324	5.092	4.876	4.675
16	14.718	13.578	12.561	11.652	10.838	10.106	9.447	8.851	8.313	7.824	7.379	6.974	6.604	6.265	5.954	5.668	5.405	5.162	4.938	4.730
17	15.562	14.292	13.166	12.166	11.274	10.477	9.763	9.122	8.544	8.022	7.549	7.120	6.729	6.373	6.047	5.749	5.475	5.222	4.990	4.775
18	16.398	14.992	13.754	12.659	11.690	10.828	10.059	9.372	8.756	8.201	7.702	7.250	6.840	6.467	6.128	5.818	5.534	5.273	5.033	4.812
19	17.226	15.679	14.324	13.134	12.085	11.158	10.336	9.604	8.950	8.365	7.839	7.366	6.938	6.550	6.198	5.877	5.584	5.316	5.070	4.843
20	18.046	16.351	14.878	13.590	12.462	11.470	10.594	9.818	9.129	8.514	7.963	7.469	7.025	6.623	6.259	5.929	5.628	5.353	5.101	4.870

Formulae

Time series

Additive model:
  Series = Trend + Seasonal + Random
Multiplicative model:
  Series = Trend * Seasonal * Random

Regression analysis

The linear regression equation of Y on X is given by:

$$Y = a + bX \text{ or } Y - \bar{Y} = b(X - \bar{X}),$$

where:

$$b = \frac{\text{Covariance } (XY)}{\text{Variance } (X)} = \frac{n\sum XY - (\sum X)(\sum Y)}{n\sum X^2 - (\sum X)^2}$$

and $a = \bar{Y} - b\bar{X}$
or solve

$$\sum Y = na + b\sum X$$
$$\sum XY = a\sum X + b\sum X^2$$

Exponential $Y = ab^x$
Geometric $Y = aX^b$

Learning curve

$$Y_x = aX^b$$

where
Y_x = the cumulative average time per unit to produce X units;
a = the time required to produce the first unit of output;
X = the cumulative number of units;
b = the index of learning.
  The exponent b is defined as the log of the learning curve improvement rate divided by log 2.

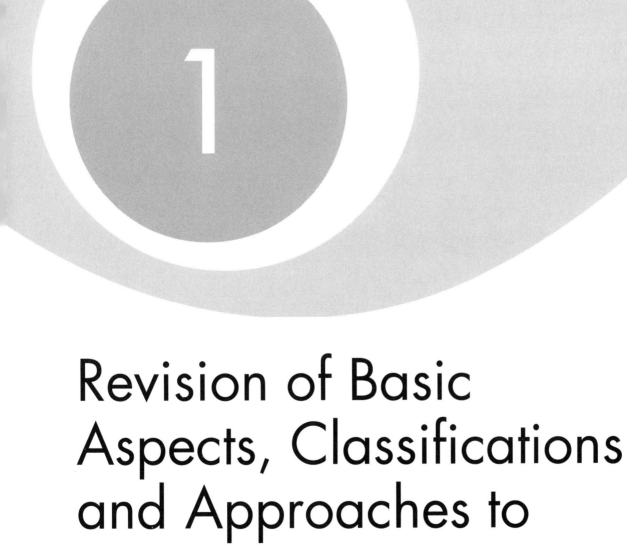

Revision of Basic Aspects, Classifications and Approaches to Cost Accounting

Revision of Basic Aspects, Classifications and Approaches to Cost Accounting

 Cost units are units of product or service for which costs are ascertained
Cost centres are locations, functions or activities for which costs are accumulated

Classification of costs

Costs can be classified by nature or purpose. When classifying by behaviour, costs can be categorised as fixed, variable, stepped fixed or semi-variable. Semi-variable costs can be analysed into their fixed and variable components using the high–low method.

The high–low method

$$\text{Total cost} = (\text{Variable cost per unit} \times \text{units made}) + \text{Fixed costs}$$

$$\text{Variable cost p/u} = \frac{\text{Cost at highest activity level} - \text{Cost at lowest activity level}}{\text{Units made at highest activity level} - \text{Units made at lowest activity level}}$$

The fixed cost can then be found by using the variable cost calculated

Total cost at (either) activity level $-$ (Variable cost p/u $\times$ units made at chosen level) = Fixed costs

Questions

1.1 Cost centres are:

  (A) units of output or service for which costs are ascertained.
  (B) functions or locations for which costs are ascertained.
  (C) a segment of the organisation for which budgets are prepared.
  (D) amounts of expenditure attributable to various activities.

3

1.2 Prime cost is:

(A) all costs incurred in manufacturing a product.
(B) the total of direct costs.
(C) the material cost of a product.
(D) the cost of operating a department.

1.3 Fixed costs are conventionally deemed to be:

(A) constant per unit of output.
(B) constant in total when production volume changes.
(C) outside the control of management.
(D) those unaffected by inflation.

1.4 The following data relate to two activity levels of an out-patient department in a hospital:

Number of consultations by patients	4,500	5,750
Overheads	£269,750	£289,125

Fixed overheads are not affected by the number of consultations per period. The variable cost per consultation:

(A) is approximately £15.50
(B) is approximately £44.44
(C) is approximately £59.94
(D) cannot be calculated without more information.

1.5 P Ltd is preparing the production budget for the next period. Based on previous experience, it has found that there is a linear relationship between production volume and production costs. The following cost information has been collected in connection with production:

Volume (units)	Cost (£)
1,600	23,200
2,500	25,000

What would be the production cost for a production volume of 2,700 units?

(A) £5,400
(B) £25,400
(C) £27,000
(D) £39,150

1.6 The following is a graph of cost against volume of output:

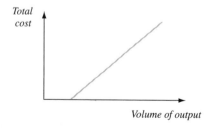

To which of the following costs does the graph correspond?

(A) Electricity bills made up of a standing charge and a variable charge.
(B) Bonus payments to employees when production reaches a certain level.

(C) Sales commission payable per unit up to a maximum amount of commission.

(D) Bulk discounts on purchases, the discount being given on all units purchased.

The following information relates to questions 1.7–1.11

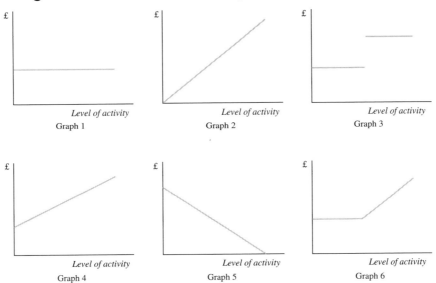

Which one of the above graphs illustrates the costs described in questions 1.7–1.11?

1.7 A linear variable cost – when the vertical axis represents cost incurred.

(A) Graph 1
(B) Graph 2
(C) Graph 4
(D) Graph 5

1.8 A fixed cost – when the vertical axis represents cost incurred.

(A) Graph 1
(B) Graph 2
(C) Graph 3
(D) Graph 6

1.9 A linear variable cost – when the vertical axis represents cost per unit.

(A) Graph 1
(B) Graph 2
(C) Graph 3
(D) Graph 6

1.10 A semi-variable cost – when the vertical axis represents cost incurred.

(A) Graph 1
(B) Graph 2
(C) Graph 4
(D) Graph 5

1.11 A step fixed cost – when the vertical axis represents cost incurred.

(A) Graph 3
(B) Graph 4
(C) Graph 5
(D) Graph 6

1.12 Over long-time periods of several years, factory rent costs will tend to behave as:

    (A) linear variable costs
    (B) fixed costs
    (C) step fixed costs
    (D) Curvilinear variable costs

✓ Answers

1.1 Answer: (B)

Cost centres act as 'collecting places' for costs before they are analysed further.

1.2 Answer: (B)

Answer (A) describes total production cost. Answer (C) is only a part of prime cost. Answer (D) is an overhead cost.

1.3 Answer: (B)

The total amount of fixed costs remains unchanged when production volume changes, therefore the unit rate fluctuates.

1.4 Answer: (A)

With the same amount of fixed overheads at both activity levels, the change in overheads must be due to extra variable cost.

	Overheads	Consultations
	£	
High	289,125	5,750
Low	269,750	4,500
Change	19,375	1,250

$$\text{Variable overhead cost per consultation} = \frac{£19,375}{1,250} = £15.50$$

1.5 Answer: (B)

Units	£
2,500	25,000
1,600	23,200
900	1,800

$$\text{Variable cost per unit} = \frac{£1,800}{900} = £2$$

Substitute in high activity:

	£
Total cost	25,000
Variable cost = 2,500 units × £2	5,000
Therefore fixed cost	20,000

Forecast for 2,700 units:

	£
Fixed cost	20,000
Variable cost 2,700 × £2	5,400
Total cost	25,400

1.6 Answer: (B)

The graph shows a variable cost which starts to be incurred only beyond a certain volume of output. Only B fits this description of cost behaviour.

1.7 Answer: (B)

Graph 2 depicts a cost which increases in total by equal amounts for each increment in the level of activity.

1.8 Answer: (A)

Graph 1 depicts a cost which remains the same regardless of the level of activity.

1.9 Answer: (A)

The variable cost per unit remains constant regardless of the level of activity.

1.10 Answer: (C)

Graph 4 depicts a cost which contains a fixed element which is incurred even at zero activity. Thereafter the cost increases in total by equal amounts for each increment in the level of activity: this is the extra variable cost incurred.

1.11 Answer: (A)

Graph 3 depicts a cost which remains constant up to a critical level of activity. At that point the total cost increases by a step to a new, higher level.

1.12 Answer: (C)

As activity increases or decreases over a period of several years the rent cost will remain constant for a range of activity but will then increase or decrease in steps as critical activity levels are reached when larger or smaller premises are needed.

Absorption Costing, Activity-based Costing and Marginal Costing

Absorption Costing, Activity-based Costing and Marginal Costing

2

Absorption costing

Where an item is costed using absorption costing, the production overheads are spread over the units produced. Costs attributable to a specific cost centre are *allocated* first, then non-specific costs are *apportioned* according to the benefit received, before the overheads are *absorbed* by the individual cost units. The absorption rate chosen should be time-based where possible.

Under- or over-absorption

Overheads may be under or over absorbed if estimated costs don't match the actual figures. The difference between the amount absorbed and the true cost is charged/credited to the income statement for the period.

Activity-based costing

An alternative method of absorbing overheads is to use activity-based costing, where costs are collected on the basis of the activities which consume resources and overheads are allocated to products on the basis of appropriate cost drivers.

For example

- Stores costs (say £20,000) may be driven by the number of requisitions raised (say 50).
- A cost per requisition can therefore be calculated (£20,000/50 = £400).
- A particular product line will therefore absorb stores costs on the basis of the number of requisitions raised in order to produce that line. So, if to produce all of Product X required 6 requisitions, then Product X would absorb £400 × 6 = £2,400 of stores costs.
- If 12,000 units of Product X were made in total, the element of stores cost in the overall unit cost of Product X would be £2,400/12,000 = £0.2.

Steps

1 Identify the activities that cause costs (cost drivers)
2 Collect costs around the drivers (cost pools)
3 Calculate the level of each activity
4 Calculate a rate for each activity
5 Allocate the costs to products.

Advantages

- Costs reflect complexity and diversity of production
- Selling prices more realistically reflect resources used by products
- Aids control
- Allocates responsibility
- Reduces arbitrary nature of cost absorption.

Disadvantages

- Complexity
- Still not 'correct' cost per unit
- Not all costs have obvious drivers
- Implies more control than really exists
- Profits are still distorted by inventory building.

Marginal costing

This values items at the variable or marginal cost only. Fixed costs are treated as period costs and are written off in full against the contribution for the period. Since the two systems value inventory differently, it follows that each will report a different profit figure for the period if inventory levels alter.

Profits can be reconciled as follows:

Marginal cost profit	x
Increase/decrease in inventory × fixed cost p/unit	x / (x)
Absorption cost profit	x

Questions

2.1 A company has budgeted production of 500 X's and 300 Y's next year. Y's take twice as long to make as X's.

Total fixed overheads are expected to be £102,000.

Costs relating to the X are budgeted at

| Materials: | 3,000 kg | £24,000 |
| Labour: | 2,000 hours | £40,000 |

Fixed overheads are to be absorbed on an hourly basis.

In addition to the above some material normally goes to waste, this is expected to amount to 10% of materials purchased.

What is the absorption cost per unit of X?

(4 marks)

2.2   A company's production and sales were budgeted at 300 units.

Actual production was 315 but sales were only 295.

The marginal cost profit was

	£	£
Sales		64,900
COS		
Materials	15,750	
Labour	15,750	
	31,500	
Closing stock	2,000	
		29,500
		35,400
Fixed overheads		9,000
Net profit		26,400

All costs were in line with expectations.
There was no opening stock.

What would the under/over absorption of overheads have been if the company had used absorption costing?

(2 marks)

2.3   A company budgeted to produce and sell equal numbers of units. In fact, production was above budget whilst sales were below budget. Is the absorption costing profit likely to be higher or lower than marginal costing profit?

(2 marks)

2.4   The following are the results of last year's production.

Budgeted overheads = £8,000
Budgeted production = 4,000 units
Actual overheads = £8,500
Actual production = 3,800 units

What is the over/under absorption?

(2 marks)

2.5   A company's cost card is shown below.

	£
Materials	10
Labour	15
Fixed overheads	8
	33
Variable selling costs	7
	40
Selling price	50
Profit	10

Last year 4,000 units were produced, of which 3,750 were sold. Actual fixed overheads were £28,000. There was no opening inventory.

Calculate the profits under marginal costing and absorption costing, and reconcile them.

(5 marks)

2.6 A company is changing its costing system from traditional absorption costing (AC) based on labour hours to ABC.

It has overheads of £156,000 which are related to taking material deliveries.

The delivery information about each product is below.

Product:	X	Y	Z
Total units required	1,000	2,000	3,000
Delivery size	200	400	1,000

Total labour costs are £360,000 for 45,000 hours. Each unit of each product takes the same number of direct hours.

Assuming that the company uses the number of deliveries as its cost driver, calculate the increase or decrease in unit costs for Z arising from the change from AC to ABC.

(3 marks)

2.7 A company uses activity-based costing to calculate the unit cost of its products. The figures for Period 3 are below.

Production set-up costs are £84,000.
Total production is 40,000 units of each of products A and B.
Each run is 2,000 units of A or 5,000 units of B.

What is the set-up cost per unit of B?

(2 marks)

2.8 DRP Ltd has recently introduced an ABC system. It manufactures three products, details of which are set out below:

Product:	D	R	P
Budgeted annual production (units)	100,000	100,000	50,000
Batch size (units)	100	50	25
Machine set-ups per batch	3	4	6
Purchase orders per batch	2	1	1
Processing time per unit (minutes)	2	3	3

Three cost pools have been identified. Their budgeted costs for the year ending 30 June 2003 are as follows:

Machine set-up costs £150,000
Purchasing of materials £70,000
Processing £80,000.

What is the budgeted machine set-up cost per unit of product R?

(3 marks)

2.9   A company makes products A and B. It is experimenting with ABC.

Production set-up costs are £12,000.
Total production will be 20,000 units of each of products A and B.
Each run is 1,000 units of A or 5,000 units of B.

What is the set-up cost per unit of A, using ABC?

(2 marks)

2.10   Which changes in the modern business environment have led to the need for ABC to replace more traditional approaches?

(5 marks)

2.11   Exe plc is a motor car manufacturer. Exe plc has been in business for many years, and it has recently invested heavily in automated processes. It continues to use a total costing system for pricing, based on recovering overheads by a labour hour absorption rate.

Exe plc is currently experiencing difficulties in maintaining its market share. It is therefore considering various options to improve the quality of its motor cars, and the quality of its service to its customers. It is also investigating its present pricing policy, which is based on the costs attributed to each motor car.

Requirements

(a)   Discuss the significance to Exe plc of developing and maintaining communication links with suppliers and customers.

(10 marks)

(b)   Explain the benefits (or otherwise) that an ABC system would give Exe plc.

(10 marks)
(Total = 20 marks)

✅ **Answers**

2.1   Note that material cost given represents only 90% of total costs and must be increased by a factor of 10/9.

The overheads must be shared between the products using labour hours (2,000 ÷ 500 = 4 hours for an X and therefore 8 hours for a Y).

	£
Material cost: £24,000 × 10/9 = £26,667	
Per unit (£26,667 ÷ 500)	53.33
Labour cost per unit (£40,000 ÷ 500)	80.00
FO per unit	
Total hours: X + Y	
500 × 4 hours + 300 × 8 hours = 4,400 hours	
Overheads per hour: £102,000 ÷ 4,400 = £23.18	
Per unit of X (£23.18 × 4 hours)	92.72
AC per unit	226.05 = B

2.2 Overheads would be over absorbed since actual production was higher than budget.

Remember to use production as a basis for absorption, not sales.

Budgeted FO per unit = £9,000 ÷ 300 units = £30.00

	£
Absorbed (£30.00 × 315)	9,450
Spent	9,000
Over absorbed	450 = D

2.3 In this case stocks will rise and thus absorption costing will carry forward some overheads to the next period.

Thus absorption costing profits will be higher.

2.4 Always work out the absorption rate before you start an absorption costing question.

Absorption rate = £8,000/4,000 = £2 per unit

Total overhead absorbed = £2 × 3,800 units = £7,600

Total amount spent = £8,500

Under absorption = £8,500 − £7,600 = £900.

2.5 Remember to value inventory correctly: include the fixed overheads only in absorption costing.

Marginal cost = £25, absorption cost = £33

	Unit	MC		AC	
	£	£	£	£	£
Sales	50		187,500		187,500
COS					
Materials	10	40,000		40,000	
Labour	15	60,000		60,000	
FO	0/8	–		32,0 00	
		100,000		132,000	
Closing inventory	25/33	(6,250)		(8,250)	
			93,750		123,750
			93,750		63,750
FO			(28,000)		
Over absorption					4,000
			65,750		67,750
Selling costs	7	(26,250)		(26,250)	
Profit			39,500		41,500

Reconciliation

	£
Profit per AC	41,500
Less: FO in closing inventory (£8 × 250 units)	(2,000)
Profit per MC	39,500

2.6   It is worth noting that the labour cost is not needed here: it is a direct cost and will not change, regardless of the method used.

We will calculate the overhead cost per unit under both systems, and calculate the difference.

AC

Since the time per unit is the same for each product, the overheads per unit will also be the same

£156,000 ÷ 6,000 units = £26

(you would get the same answer using labour hours)

ABC

Number of deliveries for X (1,000 ÷ 200)	5
Number of deliveries for Y (2,000 ÷ 400)	5
Number of deliveries for Z (3,000 ÷ 1,000)	3
Total	13

Cost per delivery = £156,000 ÷ 13 = £12,000
Cost per unit of Z = £12,000 ÷ 3,000 units = £4
Decrease = £26 − £4 = £22.

2.7   We must divide the costs by the number of set-ups to enable the costs to be shared.

Cost driver = number of set-ups
Cost pool = £84,000
Total set-ups = 20 (for A) + 8 (for B) = 28
Rate = £84,000/28 = £3,000 per set-up

Cost for A = £3,000 × 20 set-ups = £60,000
    Per unit = £60,000/40,000 = £1.50

Cost for B = £3,000 × 8 set-ups = £24,000
    Per unit = £24,000/40,000 = £0.60.

2.8   Make sure you followed the instructions and only calculated the *machine set-up cost per unit* of *R*. Much of the information was unnecessary.

Check that you understand the calculation of the total number of set-ups.

Total set-ups = Budget production ÷ batch size × set-ups per batch

D (100,000 ÷ 100 × 3)	3,000
R (100,000 ÷ 50 × 4)	8,000
P (50,000 ÷ 25 × 6)	12,000
	23,000

Cost per set-up = £150,000 ÷ 23,000 = £6.52

Therefore cost per unit of R = £6.52 × 8,000 set-ups ÷ 100,000 units = £0.52.

2.9   You need to ensure that you understand the workings of cost drivers, as shown below.

Cost driver = number of set-ups
Cost pool = £12,000
Total set-ups = 20 (for A) + 4 (for B) = 24
Rate = £12,000/24 = £500 per set-up

Cost for A = £500 × 20 set-ups = £10,000
    Per unit = £10,000/20,000 = £0.50

Cost for B = £500 × 4 set-ups = £2,000
    Per unit = £2,000/20,000 = £0.10.

2.10   Recent changes necessitating ABC include

- a proportionate increase in fixed costs making the sharing of them more significant
- the increase of flexibility and diversity, leading to extra costs associated with these factors
- increasing customer focus, leading to a wider variety of products
- increased competition, leading to the need for more realistic cost information
- the increased desire to control production systems, requiring information about what activities cause which costs.

2.11   (a)   The reasons for developing and maintaining communication links with suppliers and customers are many and varied. Five are considered below.

1   *Corporate growth.* Many companies have growth as one of their corporate objectives, often it is an integral part of achieving the profit targets that have been set. Exe plc cannot grow unless it starts to meet the needs of its customers and thus it needs to communicate with them to understand their needs and to ascertain why its market share is falling.

Approaches such as the balanced scorecard highlight the importance of the customer perspective.

2   *Costs.* Exe will have very high fixed costs due to the nature of its process (heavily automated). If volumes are below capacity this will lead to high overheads per unit. This can lead to a vicious spiral: high costs lead to high prices which lead to falling volumes leading to even higher unit costs. The only way to break out of this is to meet customer needs and increase volume. Proper communication is vital to this.

Marginal costing may appear to alleviate this but it does not solve the basic premise that high fixed cost companies require high sales.

3   *Budgeting.* A company starts to budget by identifying and anticipating the principal budget factor. For Exe this is clearly sales. Links with customers will help to identify probable sales levels in the future. This will help with capacity planning, sourcing of resources and staffing levels.

4   *Stock management.* Whether or not Exe adopts a JIT approach to production it will be looking to keep inventory at a reasonably low level: excessive inventory tie up capital, make profits look artificially high (especially with absorption costing valuations) and encourage staff to sell what is in inventory rather than discover customers' needs and supply them.

Good inventory control requires very good communication links with both suppliers and customers to properly maximise throughput.

5   *Quality.* Quality is one of the key selling points of many businesses and Exe is clearly no exception. Quality is customer defined and significantly influenced by suppliers. The introduction of a formal TQM system would reinforce the importance of quality and customer focus, but even without this Exe would get many of the benefits of customer focus.

(b) An ABC system is a form of absorption costing that dispenses with the arbitrary labour hours (or similar) as a basis for absorption and replaces it with a more realistic system based on the activities that cause the costs.

The benefits of this to Exe are set out below.

The cost split between products should be more realistic, helping to inform Exe's management as to which products are using more of the company's productive resources.

An understanding of the activities that cause costs should help the management of Exe to exercise better control over those activities, and hence the costs.

Selling prices based on cost will now more realistically reflect the resources that went into producing the car being sold, helping to ensure that Exe becomes (more) profitable.

The adoption of ABC can be part of a wider scheme encouraging everyone to focus on their customer, as required by TQM and similar approaches. It is clear that sales staff have customers, but it should also be apparent that the management accountant has customers: managers. Managers need accurate reliable relevant information to help them fulfil their roles; ABC should help provide this.

An ABC system will reflect the change in the nature of production: traditional manufacturing had a large direct labour component, and thus using labour hours to absorb overheads was realistic; a change to ABC will reinforce to management the changes in the company.

As car production becomes more customer focused and customers demand ever more personalised products, the complexity and diversity inherent in the system will be captured by the costing information.

Unfortunately ABC suffers from some drawbacks.

It implies more than it can deliver: ABC is still somewhat arbitrary. Managers may feel that this is the "correct" cost and make incorrect decisions because of this.

Activity-based costing is more complex and time-consuming than traditional approaches. It is not clear that its benefits are sufficiently high to ensure that it covers its own costs.

On balance an ABC system will probably benefit the company, but it would become much more powerful if combined with JIT and TQM production systems.

3

Breakeven Analysis

Breakeven Analysis

3

Breakeven analysis considers the level of activity in terms of sales units and sales revenue that a business requires to meet in order to breakeven.

It requires mathematical skills and the ability to draw graphs.

π Useful equations:

1   Breakeven point (in units) $= \dfrac{\text{Fixed costs}}{\text{Contribution per unit}}$

---

2   C/S ratio (Contribution/Sales ratio) $= \dfrac{\text{Contribution per unit}}{\text{Selling price per unit}}$

The C/S ratio is also known as P/V ratio (Profit/Volume ratio).

---

3   Breakeven point (in sales revenue terms) $= \dfrac{\text{Fixed costs}}{\text{C/S ratio}}$

---

4   Margin of safety $= \dfrac{\text{Budgeted sales} - \text{Breakeven sales}}{\text{Budgeted sales}} \times 100\%$

---

5   Sales required (in units) to achieve a particular profit target

$= \dfrac{\text{Fixed costs} + \text{Profit target}}{\text{Contribution per unit}}$

---

6   Sales required (in revenue terms) to achieve a particular profit target

$= \dfrac{\text{Fixed costs} + \text{Profit target}}{\text{C/S ratio}}$

You also need to be able to draw two graphs – the Breakeven chart and the Profit/Volume chart.

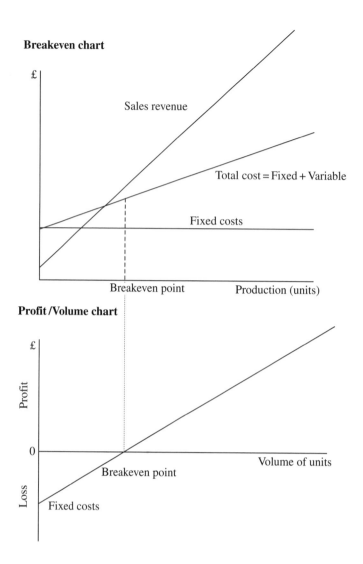

Breakeven chart

Profit/Volume chart

? Questions

3.1 DVL plc sells three products. The budgeted fixed cost for the period is £592,000. The budgeted contribution to sales ratio (C/S ratio) and sales mix are as follows:

Product	C/S ratio (%)	Mix (%)
D	27	30
V	56	20
L	38	50

What is the breakeven sales revenue?

(2 marks)

3.2 Which of the following may be required to determine the breakeven sales value in a multi-product manufacturing environment?

(i) individual product gross contribution to sales ratio
(ii) the general fixed cost
(iii) the product-specific fixed cost

    (iv)   the product mix ratio

    (v)   the method of apportionment of general fixed costs

    A   (i), (ii), (iii) and (iv) only
    B   (i), (iii) and (iv) only
    C   (i), (ii) and (iv) only
    D   All of them

(2 marks)

3.3   Edward produces a single product. For the forthcoming period, the budget contains the following information:

	£
Revenue	416,000
Fixed overheads	62,000
Contribution	104,000

What is the margin of safety in percentage terms?

(4 marks)

3.4   Thomas produces three products K, L and M. The products are usually bundled up when sold and have to be sold in the ratio 5:3:2 (K:L:M).

The contribution to sales ratios of the three products are

    K   25%
    L   30%
    M   40%

Budgeted fixed costs are £1,180,000.

What is the budgeted breakeven sales revenue?

(4 marks)

3.5

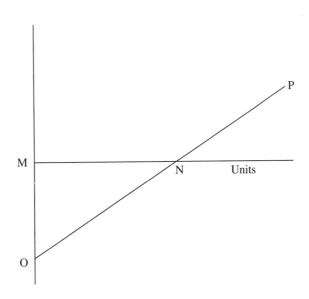

Which of the following statements is true?

	Name of graph	Breakeven point	Fixed costs
A	Breakeven chart	N	M
B	Breakeven chart	M	O
C	Profit/Volume chart	M	P
D	Profit/Volume chart	P	O
E	Profit/Volume chart	N	O

(2 marks)

3.6 The following information relates to a company making televisions:

	£
Budgeted sales revenue	1,300,000
Budgeted profit	130,000
Budgeted contribution	520,000

What is the budgeted sales revenue to breakeven?

(3 marks)

3.7 RT Ltd wants to make a profit of £595,000. It has fixed costs of £347,000 and a C/S ratio of 0.8. The product selling price is £15.

What number of units will RT Ltd have to sell in order to achieve the targeted profit?

(3 marks)

Use the following information to answer the next two questions.

HG plc manufactures four products. The unit cost and selling price details per unit are as follows:

	Product W £	Product X £	Product Y £	Product Z £
Selling price	56	67	89	96
Materials	22	31	38	46
Labour	15	20	18	24
Variable overhead	12	15	18	15
Fixed overhead	4	2	8	7

3.8 Assuming that labour is a unit variable cost, if the products are ranked according to their contribution to sales ratio, which will be the most profitable product?

(2 marks)

3.9 Assuming that labour is a unit variable cost, if budgeted unit sales are in the ratio W:2, X:3, Y:3, Z:4 and monthly fixed costs are budgeted to be £15,000, what number of units of W would be sold at the budgeted breakeven point?

(2 marks)

3.10 KLQ plc sells three products. The ratio of their total sales values is K2:L3:Q5.

The contribution to sales ratios of the products are

K 30%
L 25%
Q 50%

If fixed costs for the period are expected to be £160,000, what revenue (to the nearest £1,000) is needed to earn a marginal costing profit of £41,000?

(2 marks)

3.11 A new product will have fixed costs of £1,700,000. It will be sold for £6 with associated variable costs of £3.25. Mean sales for the coming year are estimated at 580,000 units. Sales volume is normally distributed with a standard deviation of 22,000 units. What is the probability of at least breaking-even?

(2 marks)

3.12 Foto Frames Plc. makes digital photo viewing frames which it sells to retailers for £25 per frame. Retailers typically sell the frames to consumers for £40 each.

Budgeted production for the forthcoming period is 200,000 frames. Budgeted fixed overheads are £2.4 million. Variable cost per frame is expected to be £6.50.

Retailers have started to use their buyer power over Foto Frames Plc. and have begun to demand a discount off the existing price charged to them. The directors of Foto Frames Plc. are concerned that they may lose business if they do not offer some sort of discount to their customers and have asked for advice from a market research consultancy, firm.

The consultants have suggested that Foto Frames Plc. need to decrease the selling price charged to retailers by at least 10% if they are to retain their existing customers. However, they believe that Foto Frames Plc. can use some buyer power of their own over supplier of materials such that the variable cost per frame would fall by 5%.

Requirements

(a) Calculate the breakeven point in terms of units and sales revenue, and the margin of safety based upon the existing selling price and variable cost per frame.

(3 marks)

(b) Draw the Profit/Volume chart based upon the existing selling price and variable cost per frame.

(3 marks)

(c) Calculate the breakeven point in terms of units and sales revenue, and the margin of safety, assuming the company not only decreases the selling price by 10% but also uses its own buyer power over its suppliers.

(2 marks)

(d) By how many units has the breakeven point changed?

(1 mark)
(Total = 10 marks)

3.13 Laws Stores Ltd owns a large out-of-town store selling sports equipment. For reporting and control purposes it splits the business into four product groups: Ball sports, Racquet sports, Water sports and Outdoor activities.

The board of directors is dominated by the Laws family who have heard a rumour that one of the large quoted sports goods retailers is seeking planning permission to build a new store nearby. The board of Laws Stores Ltd feel that to compete they may have to decrease the prices of their products.

For the forthcoming year, before any price changes are implemented, budgeted information is as follows:

	Ball sports £	Racquet sports £	Water sports £	Outdoor activities £
Sales	800,000	400,000	250,000	150,000
Variable costs	500,000	260,000	190,000	126,000

Fixed costs of operating the store are budgeted to be £400,000.

Price decreases are being contemplated as follows:

	Average price decrease (%)
Ball sports	10
Racquet sports	5
Water sports	6
Outdoor activities	4

Although these price decreases are expected to be needed to defend sales volume from the threat posed by new competition, the directors believe that sales volume for Water sports and Outdoor activities might even increase as a result of the lower prices being proposed.

In fact, the *sales volume* changes as a result of the decrease in prices and are expected to be as follows:

Ball sports	Unchanged if prices are decreased by 10%
Racquet sports	Unchanged if prices are decreased by 5%
Water sports	Increase of 15% if prices are decreased by 6%
Outdoor activities	Increase of 10% if prices are decreased by 4%

Requirements

(a) Calculate the C/S ratio and breakeven sales revenue for the store before any changes to product selling prices.

(4 marks)

(b) Calculate the effect upon profit of the proposed price changes and suggest whether they should be implemented. Ignore economies of scale.

(3 marks)

(c) Discuss the other factors that should be considered before implementing the proposed changes to product prices.

(3 marks)

(Total = 10 marks)

3.14 GHK (DM 5/06)

GHK manufactures four products from different combinations of the same direct materials and direct lab our. An extract from the flexible budgets for next quarter for each of these products is as follows:

Product	G		H		J		K	
Units	3,000	5,000	3,000	5,000	3,000	5,000	3,000	5,000
	$'000	$'000	$'000	$'000	$'000	$'000	$'000	$'000
Revenue	30	50	60	100	45	75	90	150
Direct material A (note 1)	9	15	12	20	4.5	7.5	18	30
Direct material B (note 2)	6	10	6	10	13.5	22.5	36	60
Direct labour (note 3)	6	10	24	40	22.5	37.5	9	15
Overhead (note 4)	6	8	13	19	11	17	11	17

Notes:

1   Material A was purchased sometime ago at a cost of $5 per kg. There are 5,000 kg in inventory. The costs shown in the flexible budget are based on this historical cost. The material is in regular use and currently has a replacement cost of $7 per kg.

2   Material B is purchased as required; its expected cost is $10 per kg. The costs shown in the flexible budget are based on this expected cost.

3   Direct labour costs are based on an hourly rate of $10 per hour. Employees work the number of hours necessary to meet production requirements.

4   Overhead costs of each product include a specific fixed cost of $1,000 per quarter which would be avoided if the product was to be discontinued. Other fixed overhead costs are apportioned between the products but are not affected by the mix of products manufactured.

GHK has been advised by the only supplier of material B that the quantity of material B that will be available during the next quarter will be limited to 5,000 kg. Accordingly, the company is being forced to reconsider its production plan for the next quarter. GHK has already entered into contracts to supply one of its major customers with the following:

500 units of product G
1,600 units of product H
800 units of product J
400 units of product K

Apart from this, the demand expected from other customers is expected to be

3,600 units of product G
3,000 units of product H
3,000 units of product J
4,000 units of product K

The major customer will not accept partial delivery of the contract and if the contract with this major customer is not completed in full, then GHK will have to pay a financial penalty of $5,000.

Requirements

(a)   For each of the four products, calculate the relevant contribution per $ of material B for the next quarter.

(6 marks)

(b)   It has been determined that the optimum production plan based on the data above is to produce 4,100 units of product G, 4600 units of product H, 800 units of product J and 2,417 units of product K. Determine the amount of financial penalty at which GHK would be indifferent between meeting the contract or paying the penalty.

(5 marks)

(c) Calculate the relevant contribution to sales ratios for each of the four products.

(2 marks)

(d) Assuming that the limiting factor restrictions no longer apply, prepare a sketch of a multi-product profit–volume chart by ranking the products according to your contribution to sales ratio calculations based on total market demand. Your sketch should plot the products using the highest contribution to sales ratio first.

(6 marks)

(e) Explain briefly, stating any relevant assumptions and limitations, how the multi-product profit–volume chart that you prepared in (d) above may be used by the manager of GHK to understand the relationships between costs, volume and profit within the business.

(6 marks)
(Total = 25 marks)

 Answers

3.1
$$\text{Budgeted breakeven sales} = \frac{\text{Budgeted fixed costs}}{\text{C/S ratio}}$$

We know the budgeted fixed costs but the C/S ratio is a little more involved since the company produces more than one product.

However, since the three products have to be sold in a given mix we can calculate the average C/S ratio as follows:

Average C/S ratio = $0.3 \times 27\% + 0.2 \times 56\% + 0.5 \times 38\% = 38.3\%$

So,
$$\text{Budgeted breakeven sales} = \frac{\text{Budgeted fixed costs}}{\text{C/S ratio}} = \frac{£592,000}{0.383} = £1,545,692$$

3.2 **A**

All of the statements are true except statement (v).

Contribution is used when calculating the breakeven point NOT profit.

Apportionment of general fixed costs would only be required if the business wished to calculate the profit generated per product for some reason.

3.3 The margin of safety is calculated as:

$$\frac{\text{Budgeted sales} - \text{Sales to breakeven}}{\text{Budgeted sales}}$$

So we need to calculate the breakeven sales revenue.

To do this we need the C/S (Contribution/Sales) ratio.

C/S ratio = £104,000/£416,000 = 25%

$$\text{Sales revenue to breakeven} = \frac{\text{Fixed costs}}{\text{C/S ratio}}$$

$$= \frac{£62,000}{0.25} = £248,000$$

$$\text{So margin of safety} = \frac{£416,000 - £248,000}{£416,000} = 40.4\%$$

3.4 $$\text{Budgeted breakeven sales} = \frac{\text{Budgeted fixed costs}}{\text{C/S ratio}}$$

We know the budgeted fixed costs but the C/S ratio is a little more involved since the company produces more than one product.

However, since the three products have to be sold in a fixed ratio we can calculate the average C/S ratio as follows:

$$\text{Average C/S ratio} = \frac{5 \times 25\% + 3 \times 30\% + 2 \times 40\%}{10}$$

$$= 29.5\%$$

$$\text{So, budgeted breakeven sales} = \frac{£1,180,000}{0.295}$$

$$= £4,000,000$$

3.5 **E**

The chart is the Profit/Volume chart which passes through the x-axis at the breakeven volume of units.

If zero units are made, the business will have no revenue and suffer no variable costs, but will still have to pay its fixed costs.

At zero units the loss would be at point "O" which is equal to the fixed costs of the business.

3.6 $$\text{Budgeted sales revenue to breakeven} = \frac{\text{Fixed costs}}{\text{C/S ratio}}$$

Fixed cost = Contribution less profit = £520,000 − £130,000 = £390,000

$$\text{C/S ratio} = \frac{£520,000}{£1,300,000} = 0.4$$

$$\text{Budgeted sales revenue to breakeven} = \frac{£390,000}{0.4} = £975,000$$

3.7 To breakeven

$$\text{Revenue} = \frac{\text{Fixed costs}}{\text{C/S ratio}}$$

To achieve a profit target

$$\text{Revenue} = \frac{\text{Fixed costs} + \text{Profit target}}{\text{C/S ratio}}$$

$$= \frac{£347,000 + £595,000}{0.8} = £1,177,500$$

Since selling price is £11 per unit, company needs to sell £1,177,500/£15 = 78,500 units.

3.8   We need to calculate the C/S ratio for each product and rank them on the grounds of highest to lowest.

	Product W £	Product X £	Product Y £	Product Z £
Contribution	7	1	15	11
Sales	56	67	89	96
C/S ratio	7/56	1/67	15/89	11/96
	= 0.125	= 0.015	= 0.169	= 0.115
Ranking	2nd	4th	1st	3rd

Remember that contribution is selling price less all variable costs. Fixed costs are not deducted.

3.9   Since the four products are to be produced in a set mix, we can consider them being produced as a "package".

That is, every time a package is produced it will consist of 2 units of W, 3 units of X, 3 units of Y and 4 units of Z.

To breakeven, sufficient packages must be produced and sold so that the contribution earned covers the fixed costs of the company.

The fixed costs are expected to be £15,000 (given in question).

So, we need to calculate contribution generated each time that a "package" is produced and sold, as follows:

Package contribution

	£
2 units of W × £7	14
3 units of X × £1	3
3 units of Y × £15	45
4 units of Z × £11	44
Total contribution	106

The number of packages that must be sold therefore is

£106 × number of packages = £15,000

So, number of packages = £15,000/£106 = 141.51 packages.

Remember that the question is asked for the number of units of product W that must be sold.

Given that there are 2 units of W in each package, the answer must be $2 \times 141.51 = 283$ units.

3.10

$$\text{Budgeted } \textit{breakeven} \text{ sales} = \frac{\text{Budgeted fixed costs}}{\text{C/S ratio}}$$

However, to achieve a *particular profit target*:

$$\text{Budgeted sales} = \frac{\text{Budgeted fixed costs} + \text{Profit target}}{\text{C/S ratio}}$$

Since the contribution generated by selling the products of the company must be high enough to cover not only the Fixed costs, but also the profit target.

We know the budgeted fixed costs and the profit target but the C/S ratio is a little more involved since the company produces more than one product.

However, since the three products have to be sold in a fixed ratio we can calculate the average C/S ratio as follows:

$$\text{Average C/S ratio} = \frac{2 \times 30\% + 3 \times 25\% + 5 \times 50\%}{10}$$

$$= 38.5\%$$

So, budgeted sales $= \dfrac{\pounds160{,}000 + \pounds41{,}000}{0.385} = \pounds522{,}078$

3.11

$$\text{The breakeven point} = \frac{\text{Fixed costs}}{\text{Contribution per unit}} = \frac{1{,}700{,}000}{6 - 3.25} = 618{,}182 \text{ units}$$

The z value for $622, 222$ units is $\dfrac{x - \mu}{\sigma} = \dfrac{618{,}182 - 580{,}000}{22{,}000} = 1.74$

From the tables, the probability that sales would be between 580,000 units and 618,182 units is 0.4591

The probability of breaking even is therefore $0.5 - 0.4591 = 0.0409$ or 4.09%

3.12

Topic being tested

Breakeven analysis

Approach

Part (a) – Calculate the breakeven volume of units using the breakeven equation.

$$\text{Breakeven volume} = \frac{\text{Fixed costs}}{\text{Contribution per unit}}$$

Breakeven sales revenue is then:
Breakeven sales volume $\times$ selling price per unit

The margin of safety is

$$\frac{\text{Budgeted sales} - \text{Breakeven sales}}{\text{Budgeted sales}} \times 100\%$$

Part (b) – Draw the Profit/Volume chart where profit is on the y-axis and volume of units is on the x-axis.

Part (c) – Calculate the breakeven volume of units and breakeven sales revenue using the same approach as in Part (a) but using the revised contribution per unit figure.

Part (d) – Compare breakeven points.

Solution

(a) To calculate the breakeven sales volume:

$$\text{Contribution per unit} \times \text{volume of units} = \text{fixed costs}$$

Therefore,

$$\text{Volume} = \frac{\text{Fixed costs}}{\text{Contribution per unit}}$$
$$= \frac{2,400,000}{25 - 6.50} = 129,730 \text{ photo frames}$$

So, breakeven sales revenue = breakeven sales volume $\times$ selling price per frame
$$= 129,730 \times £25 = £3.24\,\text{m}$$

The margin of safety is

$$\frac{\text{Budgeted sales} - \text{Breakeven sales}}{\text{Budgeted sales}} \times 100\%$$
$$= \frac{200,000 \text{ units} - 129,730 \text{ units}}{200,000 \text{ units}} \times 100\% = 35.1\%$$

That is, sales could fall below budget by 35% in volume terms before the company needs to worry about making a loss.

(b) Profit/Volume chart (P/V chart)

The Profit/Volume chart relates profit to be achieved with the volume of units to be made and sold. Two points are needed on the line in order to be able to draw the P/V chart.

If no units are made and sold, the loss will be equal to the fixed costs of £2.4 million.

If 129,730 units are made and sold, profit will be zero (129,730 units is the breakeven point from Part (a)).

Profit/Volume chart based on original selling price and variable cost per unit:

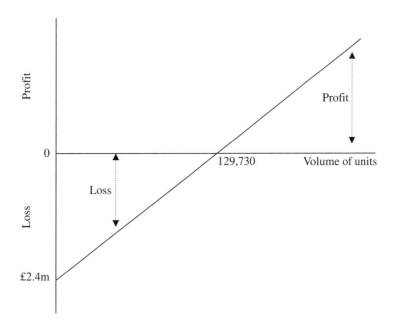

$$£$$

(c) New selling price per unit (£25 × 90%)   22.50
New variable cost per unit (£6.50 × 95%)   6.18
New contribution per unit   16.32

$$\text{New breakeven volume} = \frac{\text{Fixed costs}}{\text{Contribution per unit}}$$

$$= \frac{2,400,000}{16.32}$$

$$= 147,059 \text{ photo frames}$$

New breakeven sales revenue = 147,059 units × £22.50 = £3.31m

That is, the business needs to generate additional sales revenue of £70,000 in order to breakeven.

The new margin of safety is

$$\frac{\text{Budgeted sales} - \text{Breakeven sales}}{\text{Budgeted sales}} \times 100\%$$

$$= \frac{200,000 \text{ units} - 147,059 \text{ units}}{200,000 \text{ units}} \times 100\% = 26.5\%$$

That is, sales could now only fall by 26.5% in volume terms before the company need to worry about making a loss.

(d) The breakeven point has increased by 17,329 units in volume terms and £70,000 in sales revenue terms.

3.13

> *Topic being tested*
>
> Breakeven analysis for a multi-product company (in this question, four product types).
>
> *Approach*
>
> Part (a) – Calculate the C/S ratio (also known as the P/V ratio).
>
> $$\text{C/S ratio} = \frac{\text{Contribution for the store}}{\text{Sales revenue for the store}}$$
>
>   – Calculate breakeven sales revenue using
>
> $$\text{breakeven sales revenue} = \frac{\text{Fixed costs}}{\text{C/S ratio}}$$
>
> Part (b) – Calculate the effect upon profit by calculating the budgeted profit before the price changes are implemented and then recalculate profit once the prices have been changed.
>
>   – Conclude whether prices should be changed.
>
> Part (c) – Discuss other factors (other than the effect upon profit) that should be considered before the prices are changed.

Solution

(a)

	Ball sports £	Racquet sports £	Water sports £	Outdoor activities £
Sales	800,000	400,000	250,000	150,000
Variable costs	500,000	260,000	190,000	126,000
Contribution	300,000	140,000	60,000	24,000

Total sales revenue = £1,600,000

Total contribution = £524,000

So, C/S ratio = £524,000/£1,600,000 = 0.3275

That is, for every £1 of sales revenue generated by the store, contribution (on average) is 32.75 pence.

$$\text{Breakeven sales revenue} = \frac{\text{Fixed costs}}{\text{C/S ratio}}$$
$$= \frac{£400,000}{0.3275} = £1,221,374$$

This is 76.3% of the budgeted revenue.

(£1,221,374/£1,600,000 × 100% = 76.3%)

(b) Effect upon profit of proposed changes in selling prices:

Profit before price changes   £

Total contribution (from solution for part (a))   524,000
Less: Budgeted fixed costs   (400,000)
Budgeted profit before price changes   124,000

Profit after price changes

	Ball sports £	Racquet sports £	Water sports £	Outdoor activities £
Sales (W1)	720,000	380,000	270,250	158,400
Variable costs (W2)	500,000	260,000	218,500	138,600
Contribution	220,000	120,000	51,750	19,800

Total contribution   £411,550
Less: Budgeted fixed costs   (£400,000)

Budgeted profit after price changes   £11,550

Conclusion

Budgeted profit is expected to fall by £112,450 if the price changes being proposed are implemented.

On profit grounds, therefore, the price changes should not be implemented.

Workings

	Ball sports £	Racquet sports £	Water sports £	Outdoor activities £
W1: Sales revenue				
Sales (W1)	800,000	400,000	250,000	150,000
	× 90%	× 95%	× 115%	× 110%
			× 94%	× 96%
	= 720,000	= 380,000	= 270,250	= 158,400
W2: Variable costs				
Sales (W1)	unchanged	unchanged	190,000	126,000
			× 115%	× 110%
			= 218,500	= 138,600

(c) Other factors, that should be considered before implementing the proposed changes to product prices, would include:

Rumour relating to new entrant

How likely is it that the rumour is correct relating to the large competitor setting up nearby, is planning permission likely to be granted to them, and how long would it take before their new store would become operational.

Customer loyalty

Is there any customer loyalty amongst local customers such that less dramatic price changes may be possible to stave off the effects of a new local competitor.

Economies of scale

What size of store would the quoted sports goods retailer be likely to open and what cost benefits might they achieve from having a larger store than that of Laws Stores Ltd. (These cost benefits might come in the form of buyer power to demand discounts from their suppliers, perhaps a rent-free period for the early years if the store is to be rented rather than owned, and so on.)

Specialisation

Would it be possible for Laws Stores Ltd to sell a narrower range of sports goods than at present and compete by being seen to be the specialist provider for the local area and beyond.

3.14

Topic being tested

The question requires you to use relevant cost principles to calculate the relevant contributions for each of four products from the data provided in part (a), to calculate in part (b) the sensitivity of the product mix solution provided to a change in a financial penalty and in parts (c), (d) and (e) of the question to prepare a multi-product profit–volume chart and discuss its assumptions and limitations.

Approach

(a) Determine the relevant product contributions. Calculate the relevant contribution per $ of material B

(b) Calculate the contribution from the minimum contract. Calculate the contribution from the alternative use of resources. Calculate the penalty value

(c) Calculate the product contribution/sales ratios

(d) Calculate and plot the general fixed costs. Plot the products, starting with the product which earns the highest C/S ratio

(e) Explain the use of the chart

Solution

(a) Relevant contribution per unit

Product	G	H	J	K
	$	$	$	$
Selling Price	10.00	20.00	15.00	30.00
Relevant costs				
Direct material A	4.20	5.60	2.10	8.40
Direct material B	2.00	2.00	4.50	12.00
Direct labour	2.00	8.00	7.50	3.00
Overhead	1.00	3.00	3.00	3.00
	9.20	18.60	17.10	26.40
Relevant contribution	0.80	1.40	(2.10)	3.60
Relevant contribution per $	0.40	0.70	(0.47)	0.30
of material B				

(b) If the contract were not to be completed the material B released would be as follows:

Product	Units	Material B (kg) *per unit*	Total (kg)
G	500	0.20	100
H	1,600	0.20	320
J	800	0.45	360
K	400	1.20	480
Total material B released			**1,260**

Products G and H are already being manufactured to satisfy all of the market demand, and product J has a negative relevant contribution per unit so no further production of product J is worthwhile. Therefore, the resources released would be used to increase the production of product K.

The non-contract demand for product K is 4,000 units of which 1,983 units are currently unsatisfied (4,000 − 2,017). These 1,983 units would require more material B than is released from the contract so the maximum additional units of product K that could be manufactured is 1,050 units.

The relevant contribution that would be earned from 1,050 units of product K is $3,780 (1,050 × $3.60) whereas the contract yields a gross contribution of $2,400 (see below).

Product	Units	Contribution per unit ($)	Total ($)
G	500	0.80	400
H	1,600	1.40	2,240
J	800	(2.10)	(1,680)
K	400	3.60	1,440
Total			**2,400**

From this $1,000 specific fixed cost must be deducted as this would be avoided if product J were not produced so the net relevant contribution from the contract is $1,400. Therefore, if the penalty were to be $2,380, the relevant contribution from the additional units of product K less the penalty that would then be payable would be the same as the net relevant contribution from the contract.

(c) The contribution to sales (C/S) ratios of each of the four products based on their relevant contributions is:

G 8%, H 7%, J (14%), K 12%

(d) The general fixed cost attributed to the products excluding their specific fixed costs is

Product	$
G	2,000
H	3,000
J	1,000
K	1,000
	7,000
Plus specific fixed cost	4,000
	11,000

Therefore if there were to be zero sales there would be a loss of $7,000.

Workings for chart:

Selling products with highest C/S ratios first

	Profit $	Sales $
No products	(7,000)	Nil
Start K	(8,000)	
K only	7,840	132,000
Start G	6,840	
K and G only	10,120	173,000
Start H	9,120	
K, G and H	15,560	265,000
Start J	14,560	
All	6,580	322,000

See chart.

Multi-product profit–volume chart

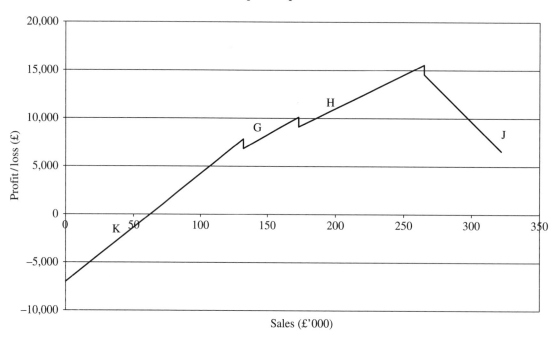

Sales (£'000)

Examiner's note:
While the chart is drawn to scale, candidates were only required to prepare a sketch.

(e) The chart shows the effect on the breakeven sales values of alternative sales mixes based on the production plan and using relevant cost. It assumes that all of the products are sold in relation to their contribution to sales ratios, highest first. Any other order of selling the units will result in a different breakeven sales value. The value indicated is the lowest breakeven sales value, the highest will occur if the products were sold in the opposite order, that is lowest contribution to sales ratio first.

The manager can use this information to understand the effect on profitability of selling the different products. Some are more worthwhile than others as demonstrated by the solution to part (a) where the products' contribution per unit were calculated and the gradient of their lines. The higher the gradient, the greater is the product's contribution to sales ratio. It can clearly be seen that sales of product J are not financially viable. It had a negative contribution to sales ratio and its line is downward sloping. Its continued production needs to be justified on other grounds. The length of each line indicates the value of sales achieved by that product.

The manager can see that if no products were sold at all the business would make a loss (due to the general fixed costs), and that when the production of a product starts there is a further reduction in profit (increase in loss) due to the product's specific fixed cost, but as products that have positive unit contributions are sold these costs are covered by the contribution from the products.

4

Relevant Cost and Short-term Decisions

Relevant Cost and Short-term Decisions

4

When making decisions, businesses should only take into account those costs and revenues which are relevant to the decision. This principle underpins virtually all of the syllabus.

Typical decisions could relate to

- The minimum price to tender for a new contract or a piece of work.
- Whether to shut down a division or keep it open.
- The minimum price to accept from a customer who requires a product which will require transfer of resources away from more profitable uses.
- Whether a manufacturing company should make for itself or buy in a component used in production of a product in its product range.

A *general rule* can be applied when attempting relevant costing questions.

General rule: "Items of income or expense are only relevant to the decision if they make the business *richer* or *poorer* when the business goes ahead with the decision."

For example, *non-cash items* are non-relevant (such as depreciation of fixed assets), since to become *richer* the business must receive cash as a result of their decision and to become *poorer* the business must spend cash.

This would also help to explain the concept of *opportunity cost* – where *another opportunity* is foregone if the business goes ahead with the decision under consideration. The amount by which they would be *poorer* is relevant and is called the *opportunity cost*.

It is important that you know which revenues and costs are relevant and which are non-relevant:

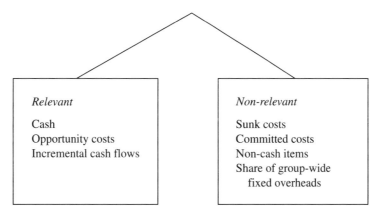

Relevant	*Non-relevant*
Cash	Sunk costs
Opportunity costs	Committed costs
Incremental cash flows	Non-cash items
	Share of group-wide fixed overheads

? Questions

4.1 Which of the following phrases are characteristics of relevant costs used for decision-making?

   (i)   Apportioned costs
   (ii) Sunk costs
   (iii) Incremental costs
   (iv) Future costs

(2 marks)

Use the following information to answer the next two questions.

Realtor Ltd is about to tender for a contract.

The following information has been provided by the company accountant.

	£
Labour required	
Fully trained (200 hours at £10/hour)	2,000
Part-trained (60 hours at £7.00/hour)	420
New joiners (400 hours at £6/hour)	2,400
Material required	
R (150 kg at £5/kg)	600
T (250 litres at £8/litre)	2,000
	7,420

Fully trained staff are currently idle. However, the new joiners will have to be diverted from another project which currently generates contribution of £12 per unit, where each unit uses four hours of their time. Part-trained workers will be recruited from outside the company if the contract is awarded to Realtor.

The original purchase price of material R was £4 per kg. If purchased now, it will cost £8 per kg. It could be sold as scrap for £2.50 per kg. Current stock is 80 kg.

Material R has not been used in the company for as long as anyone can remember.

The original purchase price of material T was £8 per litre. If purchased now, it will cost £10 per litre. It could be sold as scrap for £3.50 per litre. Current stock is 50 litres and this material is in constant use.

4.2 What is the relevant cost of labour for the contract?

(4 marks)

4.3 What is the relevant cost of materials for the contract?

(4 marks)

4.4 A company makes three products XX, YY and ZZ. The following information is available

	XX	YY	ZZ
	£	£	£
Sales	18,000	40,000	68,000
Variable costs	10,000	35,000	48,000
Fixed costs	5,000	9,000	14,000
Profit/(Loss)	3,000	(4,000)	6,000

It is believed that a percentage of the fixed costs relating to product YY are avoidable.

What is the minimum percentage of fixed costs that must be avoidable if the company is to cease producing product YY. Calculate to the nearest whole percentage.

(3 marks)

4.5 Hulme has three divisions. Budgeted information for the forthcoming period is as follows:

	Division T	Division H	Division E	Total
	£'000	£'000	£'000	£'000
Sales	700	560	150	1,550
Variable costs	550	440	100	1,090
Contribution	150	120	50	460
Fixed costs				450
Profit				10

Eighty per cent of the fixed costs are specific to each division being split between T, H and E in the ratio 3:4:1, respectively.

Which divisions should be kept open by Hulme given that their objective is to maximise profit?

(3 marks)

4.6 X plc intends to use relevant costs as the basis of the selling price for a special order: the printing of a brochure. The brochure requires a particular type of paper that is not regularly used by X plc although a limited amount is in X plc's inventory which was left over from a previous job. The cost when X plc bought this paper last year was $15 per ream and there are 100 reams in inventory. The brochure requires 250 reams. The current market price of the paper is $26 per ream, and the resale value of the paper in inventory is $10 per ream.

What is the relevant cost of the paper to be used in printing the brochure?

(2 marks)

Use the following information to answer the next two questions.

T plc manufactures a component D12, and two main products F45 and P67. The following details relate to each of these items:

	D12 $ per unit	F45 $ per unit	P67 $ per unit
Selling price	–	146.00	159.00
Material cost	10.00	15.00	26.00
Component D12 (bought-in price)	–	25.00	25.00
Direct labour	5.00	10.00	15.00
Variable overheads	6.00	12.00	18.00
Total variable cost per unit	21.00	62.00	84.00
Fixed overhead costs:	$ per annum	$ per annum	$ per annum
Avoidable*	9,000	18,000	40,000
Non-avoidable	36,000	72,000	160,000
Total	45,000	90,000	200,000

* The avoidable fixed costs are product-specific fixed costs that would be avoided if the product or component were to be discontinued.

4.7 Assuming that the annual demand for component D12 is 5,000 units and that T plc has sufficient capacity to make the component itself, what is the maximum price that should be paid to an external supplier for 5,000 components per year?

(2 marks)

4.8 Assuming that component D12 is bought from an external supplier for $25.00 per unit, what number of units of product F45 that must be sold to cover its own costs without contributing to T plc's non-avoidable fixed costs?

(2 marks)

4.9 You are currently in employment earning £25,000 per annum. You have decided to go into business for yourself doing PC repairs for local companies and will operate out of a unit available for rent at the edge of the town.

How should (i) your current salary and (ii) the rent of the unit be treated when deciding whether or not to start the business?

A (i) as an irrelevant cost and (ii) as an opportunity cost
B (i) as a sunk cost and (ii) as an committed cost
C (i) as an incremental cost and (ii) as an opportunity cost
D (i) as a committed cost and (ii) as a sunk cost
E (i) as an opportunity cost and (ii) as an incremental cost

(2 marks)

4.10   Rightlight Ltd is an advertising company and has been asked to tender for a contract to increase public awareness of global environmental issues as part of the government's commitment to improving the country's eco-footprint.

Rightlight Ltd believes that the campaign work will take a period of six months.

Five advertising specialists would need to be recruited on an annual salary of £45,000. A project manager would be needed to coordinate the campaign. An existing project manager would be used whose annual salary is currently £55,000. He would be expected to devote 30% of his time on the new contract.

The new employees would have to go through a "Environmental Awareness" training programme in order to get approval to work on government contracts. This would cost £3,000 per employee, but it is anticipated that a grant of 20% towards this cost will be available.

Alternatively, Rightlight Ltd could subcontract the work (with the government's agreement) to another PR that it sometimes uses for joint venture projects. It is anticipated that the subcontract firm would demand a fee of £135,000 to undertake the work.

What would be the relevant cost of labour for this contract?

(3 marks)

4.11   Right-Tyres Ltd has three depots selling car tyres. The depots are based in Nottingham, Luton and Manchester.

The average selling price per tyre is £25.

Budgets have been produced for the forthcoming period as follows:

	Nottingham £	Luton £	Manchester £
Sales	2,000,000	1,500,000	2,500,000
Costs:			
Purchase price of tyres	1,200,000	900,000	see below
Wages and salaries	250,000	220,000	358,000
Overheads	450,000	430,000	600,000
	1,900,000	1,550,000	see below

The average purchase price per tyre charged by suppliers is the same for both the Nottingham and Luton depots. However, due to a higher volume of tyres being purchased by the Manchester depot, the Manchester depot benefits from a 20% discount compared to the price charged to the Nottingham and Luton depots.

The management of Right-Tyres Ltd believes that some of the overheads included in the above budgets would not be incurred if the decision was taken to close any of the depots.

At a recent board meeting, doubt was cast over the future of the Luton depot given its budgeted loss of £50,000.

The percentage of overheads which are variable costs and would not be incurred if a depot were to be closed differs with each depot and are as follows:

Depot %

Nottingham 25
Luton 15
Manchester 20

If a depot were to be closed it is not expected that there would be any major consequences upon the sales volumes achieved at the remaining depots due to the geographical distances between the depots.

Requirements

(a) Discuss whether the Luton depot should be closed purely on the basis of financial considerations.

(2 marks)

(b) Assuming that 80% of wages and salaries at each depot are variable costs, calculate the number of tyres that must be sold by the whole company in order to breakeven. (For this requirement, assume that the Luton depot will be kept open and that sales will be made at the depots in the ratio used in the original budget.)

(5 marks)

(c) Discuss the key non-financial factors that should be considered when making a decision to close part of a business such as the Luton depot.

(3 marks)
(Total = 10 marks)

4.12 Relco plc is a construction company which has been asked to submit a tender to build a new hotel for a well-known national hotels group based in the UK. The specification for the hotel is as follows.

Six floors including ground floor reception and meeting rooms.
Seventy bedrooms all of similar layout and size.

A team of 100 construction workers are expected to be required to complete the project in the 18 months allowed by the specification of the project.

These workers would be sourced as follows.

Newly recruited: 50 workers, annual wages: £25,000 per annum.

Currently employed by Relco plc but not being used on any construction projects: 35 workers, annual wages: £28,000 per annum.

Currently employed, by Relco plc on another project building a new shopping centre: 15 workers, annual wages: £30,000 per annum. These 15 workers would be transferred to the hotel project but this will delay the completion of the shopping centre. Relco plc expect that this delay will cause them to have to suffer a penalty of £1.5 million for going beyond the agreed completion date, as well as additional labour costs of £300,000.

Materials are expected to cost £2.1 million and will be purchased from the company's usual suppliers if the tender is awarded to Relco plc. Suppliers typically offer 10% trade discounts to Relco plc.

Specialist equipment such as lifting gear, cement mixers and so on will be required.

Some equipment which is already owned by Relco plc and has a net book value of £500,000 would be used. The company's depreciation policy for equipment is 25% on a reducing balance basis. This equipment is not expected to be required on other projects throughout the next 18 months and beyond. It could be sold now for £600,000. Other equipment will have to be hired at an expected hire cost of £30,000 per month.

The roof of the hotel included in the specification must be strong enough to support the weight of a helicopter as planning permission has already been given for a helipad on top of the building. The materials required for the roof have not been included in the cost set out above. The only viable source of supply of these materials is a company called Helimats GmbH based in Germany who would charge around €600,000.

The exchange rate between the Euro and Sterling is currently £1 = €1.40.

Relco plc typically adds a 35% mark-up on relevant costs to arrive at a tender price.

Requirements

(a) Estimate the tender price for the hotel project with explanatory notes setting out the reasoning behind numbers used. Ignore the time value of money.

(6 marks)

(b) Discuss other factors that should be taken into account when deciding upon the tender price.

(4 marks)
(Total = 10 marks)

4.13 MOV plc (IDEC 5/03)

MOV plc produces custom-built sensors. Each sensor has a standard circuit board (SCB) in it. The current average contribution from a sensor is £400. MOV plc's business is steadily expanding and in the year just ending (2001/02), the company will have produced 55,000 sensors. The demand for MOV plc's sensors is predicted to grow over the next three years:

Year	*Units*
2002/03	58,000
2003/04	62,000
2004/05	65,000

The production of sensors is limited by the number of SCBs the company can produce. The present production level of 55,000 SCBs is the maximum that can be produced without overtime working. Overtime could increase annual output to 60,500, allowing production of sensors to also increase to 60,500. However, the variable cost of SCBs produced in overtime would increase by £75 per unit.

Because of the pressure on capacity, the company is considering having the SCBs manufactured by another company, CIR plc. This company is very reliable and produces products of good quality. CIR plc has quoted a price of £116 per SCB, for orders greater than 50,000 units a year.

MOV plc's own costs per SCB are predicted to be:

	£
Direct material	28
Direct labour	40
Variable overhead	20 (based on labour cost)
Fixed overhead	24 (based on labour cost and output of 55,000 units)
Total cost	112

The fixed overheads directly attributable to SCBs are £250,000 a year; these costs will be avoided if SCBs are not produced. If more than 59,000 units are produced, SCBs' fixed overheads will increase by £130,000.

In addition to the above overheads, MOV plc's fixed overheads are predicted to be:

Sensor production, in units:	54,001 – 59,000	59,001 – 64,000	64,001 – 70,000
Fixed overhead:	£2,600,000	£2,900,000	£3,100,000

MOV plc currently holds a stock of 3,500 SCBs but the production manager feels that a stock of 8,000 should be held if they are bought-in; this would increase stockholding costs by £10,000 a year. A purchasing officer, who is paid £20,000 a year, spends 50% of her time on SCB duties. If the SCBs are bought-in, a liaison officer will have to be employed at a salary of £30,000 in order to liase with CIR plc and monitor the quality and supply of SCBs. At present, 88 staff are involved in the production of SCBs at an average salary of £25,000 a year: if the SCBs were purchased, 72 of these staff would be made redundant at an average cost of £4,000 per employee.

The SCB department, which occupies an area of 240 × 120 square metres at the far end of the factory, could be rented out at a rent of £45 per square metre a year. However, if the SCBs were to be bought-in, for the first year only MOV plc would need the space to store the increased inventory caused by outsourcing, until the main stockroom had been reorganised and refurbished. From 2003/04, the space could be rented out; this would limit the annual production of sensors to 60,500 units. Alternatively, the space could be used for the production of sensors, allowing annual output to increase to 70,000 units if required.

Requirements

(a) Critically discuss the validity of the following statement. It was produced by Jim Elliott, the company's accountant, to show the gain for the coming year (2002/03) if the SCBs were to be bought-in.

Saving in:	£
Manufacturing staff – salaries saved: 72 staff × £25,000	1,800,000
Purchasing officer – time saved	10,000
Placing orders for SCB materials: 1,000 orders × £20 per order	20,000
Transport costs for raw materials for SCBs	45,000
Cost saved	1,875,000
Additional cost per SCB: (£116 − £112) × 58,000 units	232,000
Net gain if SCBs purchased	1,643,000

(10 marks)

(b) (i) Produce detailed calculations that show which course of action is the best financial option for the three years under consideration. (Ignore the time value of money.)

(12 marks)

(ii) Advise the company of the long-term advantages and disadvantages of buying-in SCBs.

(3 marks)
(Total = 25 marks)

Answers

4.1 Any decision to be taken must be based only on an assessment of relevant costs. Relevant items are those items of revenue and cost which will make the business either richer or poorer.

They must relate to the future and be consequences of the business going ahead with the decision. Apportioned costs relate to costs already incurred in the company and will not make the business any poorer than it would have been, had the decision not been made, and sunk costs have already affected the wealth of the business.

Relevant costs are those which will have an incremental effect upon the wealth of the business.

4.2 The relevant cost of labour is

- *Trained labour.* Skilled labour is currently idle and can therefore be transferred to the new contract at no extra cost to the business.
- *Part-trained labour.* This labour will be recruited if the contract goes ahead at a cost of £420.
- *New joiners.* This labour will have to be diverted from another project. The contribution currently being generated will therefore be foregone. The new contract will have to generate the lost contribution to ensure that the company does not suffer.

So cost for unskilled labour is

	£
Cost 400 hours at £6/hour	2,400
Contribution foregone £12 × 100 units	1,200
(400 hours/4 hour = 100 units of lost contribution)	

Total labour cost = £420 + £2,400 + £1,200 = £4,020.

4.3 The relevant cost of material R is as follows:

150 kg are needed if we win the contract of which 80 kg is in stock.

Therefore the company will have to buy 70 kg at a current purchase cost of £8/kg = £560.

The 80 kg in stock will be used for the contract. However, the company will no longer be able to sell this 80 kg for scrap proceeds of: 80 kg × £2.50 = £200.

So, relevant cost of material R is: £560 + £200 = £760.

The relevant cost of material T is as follows:

250 litres are needed if we win the contract of which 50 litres is in stock.

Therefore the company will have to buy 200 litres at a current purchase cost of £10/litre = £2,000.

The 50 litres in stock will be used for the contract. However, the company will then have to replace those 50 litres since they are needed in order to be used elsewhere in the business.

To replace these 50 litres will cost £10/litre, that is, 50 × £10 = £500.

So, relevant cost of material T is as follows: £2,000 + £500 = £2,500.

Total relevant cost of materials = £760 + £2,500 = £3,260.

4.4 It would appear that the company should cease producing product YY since it generates a loss. However, for decision-making, contribution should always be used instead of profit.

If the entire £9,000 of fixed cost is avoidable then the company should cease producing N since it will forego contribution of £5,000 but save fixed costs of £9,000 so being £4,000 better off overall.

If, say, only £4,000 of the fixed costs are avoidable, ceasing production of YY would result in loss of contribution of £5,000 but save fixed costs of £4,000 so the company would be £1,000 worse off. Here they should continue production of YY. Since contribution from YY is £5,000 at a minimum the avoidable fixed cost would have to be £5,000.

As a percentage this is £5,000/£9,000 × 100% = 56%.

4.5 If a division is closed the company will forego any contribution it was expected to generate but it will save any fixed cost that is incurred specifically by that division (no division, no specific fixed cost!).

Therefore, we must look at contribution with less specific fixed costs for each division to see what will be foregone if the division is closed.

	Division T £'000	Division H £'000	Division E £'000
Contribution	150	120	50
Specific fixed costs	(135)	(180)	(45)
(80% × 450 = 360, 360/8 × 3, 4, 1)			
	15	(60)	5

So, if Division T were to be closed the company will forego £15,000.

If Division E were closed the company will forego £5,000.

Therefore, both of these divisions should be kept open.

However, if Division H is closed the company will forego £120,000 of contribution but save specific fixed costs of £180,000 – a net saving of £60,000.

So, Division H should be closed.

4.6   100 reams @ resale value of $10 $1,000
      150 reams @ market price of $26 $3,900
                                      $4,900

4.7   This question is testing the "make or buy" decision. The business should choose to do whichever is the cheaper of the two options.

If component D12 is purchased from an external supplier, the maximum it should be prepared to pay is equal to the cost it would incur in making the component itself.

Making component D12 itself cost the business $21.00 per unit (this being the marginal cost of making each unit) although the avoidable fixed costs of $9,000. If the component were not manufactured in-house the fixed costs of $9,000 would not be incurred.

So cost of manufacturing 5,000 units of D12 = $9,000 + $21.00 × 5,000 = $114,000.

This is therefore the maximum amount that the company should be prepared to pay an external supplier.

4.8   If the component D12 is bought-in at a cost of $25 per unit, the contribution made by the business from each unit if F45 sold will be:

	$
Selling price	146
Less:	
Variable costs	(62)
(includes the $25 for component D12)	
Contribution	84

The avoidable fixed costs associated with making F45 are $18,000.

(The question asked for the number of units of product F45 that must be sold to cover its own costs without contributing to T plc's non-avoidable fixed costs, that is, to cover the avoidable fixed costs only.)

To cover this cost the business must produce the following number of units of F45:

$18,000/$84 = 214.29 units.

So, 214 units to the nearest.

4.9   **E**

By setting up your own business you will be giving up the *opportunity* to earn £30,000 per annum. The salary is therefore an opportunity cost. By taking on the rent of the business unit you will be increasing your cost base – so the rent is an incremental cost.

A committed cost is a cost which the new business is already obliged to pay (perhaps for contractual reasons). Sunk costs are past costs. Irrelevant costs are those that have no bearing on the decision to be taken.

4.10   If the contract were to go ahead, five new employees will have to be recruited at an incremental cost of 5 × £45,000 = £225,000 per annum.

This cost would only be for six months.

So cost to the contract would be: £225,000 × 0.5 = £112,500

The cost of the project manager is irrelevant since he already works for Rightlight Ltd. His salary is therefore a committed cost – even the 30% of time he will spend on the contract!

The "Environmental Awareness" training programme would cost:

5 employees × £3,000 × 80% = £12,000

So total relevant cost if Rightlight Ltd were to run the campaign would be:

£112,500 + £12,000 = £124,500

Instead, Rightlight Ltd could subcontract the work at a cost of £135,000.

The cheaper option is to employ and train the five new employees. Hence, relevant cost of labour for the contract is £124,500.

4.11

 Topic being tested

Relevant costing for decision-making

– Whether to close or keep open an apparently unprofitable part of the business.

Approach

Part (a) – Always use *contribution* not profit for decision-making purposes.
Part (b) – For breakeven calculations where a company has multiple products sold in a fixed ratio, use a "package" made up of those products in the fixed ratio.
Part (c) – Use common sense to think of non-financial consequences of shutting down part of a business in a local area.

Solution

(a) When considering shutting down part of a business it is necessary to consider the financial and non-financial effects upon the business of the closure.

The financial consequences would be as follows.

If the Luton depot is closed then sales revenue of £1.5 million will be forgone.

However, tyres cost of £900,000, wages and salaries of £220,000 and 15% of overheads (15% × £430,000 = £64,500) would no longer be incurred.

That is, the business would forgo contribution of:

	£
Sales	1,500,000
Tyres cost	(900,000)
Wages and salaries	(220,000)
Overheads	(64,500)
Contribution forgone	315,500

Eighty five per cent of the overheads, that is, £365,500 would still be incurred.

If kept open, the Luton depot will contribute £315,500 towards these overheads.

If the depot were to be closed the loss would be £365,500 rather than £50,000 if it is kept open.

Therefore, the Luton depot should be kept open.

(b)   In the original budget the number of tyres to be sold at each depot is as follows:

	Nottingham	Luton	Manchester
Sales	£2,000,000	£1,500,000	£2,500,000
Selling price	£25	£25	£25
Sale of tyres	80,000 units	60,000 units	100,000 units

This is in the ratio 8:6:10

Contribution per tyre sold at each depot will be:

	Nottingham £	Luton £	Manchester £
Selling price	25	25	25
Tyres cost:			
$\frac{£1,200,000}{80,000 \text{ units}}$	(15)	(15) (as Nottingham)	(12) (£15 × 80%)
Wages and salaries:			
$\frac{£250,000 \times 80\%}{80,000 \text{ units}}$	(2.50)		
$\frac{£220,000 \times 80\%}{60,000 \text{ units}}$		(2.93)	
$\frac{£358,000 \times 80\%}{100,000 \text{ units}}$			(2.86)
Variable overheads:			
$\frac{£450,000 \times 25\%}{80,000 \text{ units}}$	(1.41)		
$\frac{£430,000 \times 15\%}{60,000 \text{ units}}$		(1.07)	
$\frac{£600,000 \times 20\%}{100,000 \text{ units}}$			(1.20)
Contribution	6.09	6.00	8.94

Consider a "package" made up of eight tyres sold by Nottingham, six tyres sold by Luton depot and 10 tyres sold by Manchester depot (24 tyres in total).

Contribution per package would be:

		£
Nottingham	8 tyres × £6.09	48.72
Luton	6 tyres × £6.00	36.00
Manchester	10 tyres × £8.94	89.40
	24 tyres	174.12

Budgeted fixed overheads are:

		£
Nottingham	75% × £450,000	337,500
Luton	85% × £430,000	365,500
Manchester	80% × £600,000	480,000
		1,183,000

To breakeven, the number of packages comes from:

Number of packages × contribution per package = fixed costs

That is, number of packages × £174.12 = £1,183,000

So, number of packages $= \dfrac{£1,183,000}{£174.12}$

$$= 6,794.2$$

Say, 6,795 packages.

So total number of tyres that must be sold by the whole company in order to breakeven is

6,795 packages × 24 tyres = 163,080 tyres

(c) Key *non-financial* factors that should be considered when making a decision to close part of a business would include:

- The possible need for redundancies – the effect upon the morale of employees at the depots not being closed and their fear that their depot may be closed at a later date.
- Possible impact upon the brand name of the business and how the business is perceived by customers, suppliers and people in the local community.
- Possible erosion of market share if the closure were to allow a competitor to increase sales, say in Luton, and so gain a larger presence in the UK market.
- Possible bad press for the business.

4.12

 Topic being tested

The relevant costs to be considered when making a decision regarding a tender price and other non-financial factors that should be considered.

Approach

Part (a) – Read the information carefully and produce a table setting out the relevant costs together with supporting notes explaining which amounts are relevant to the decision and which are not relevant.

Part (b) – Discuss the other non-financial factors that should also be considered. Use common sense here.

Time pressure in such questions typically affects the numerical parts of the question rather than the written part which can usually be answered quickly once you have read the scenario and quickly jotted down some ideas on a plan.

Why not answer part (b) first!

Solution

(a) Statement of relevant costs for hotel project so as to derive a tender price:

	Note	£m	£m
Construction workers			
• new recruits	1	1.875	
• employees not being used	2	–	
• employees from shopping centre project	3	1.800	
			3.675
Materials	4		1.890
Equipment already owned	5	0.600	
Equipment to be hired	6	0.540	
			1.140
Materials for roof	7		0.429
			7.134
35% mark-up			2.497
Tender price			9.631

So the tender price for the hotel project should be £9.631 million.

Supporting notes

Note 1: New recruits

Fifty workers will have to be employed at an incremental cost of:

$$50 \text{ workers} \times £25{,}000 \text{ per annum} \times \frac{18 \text{ months}}{12 \text{ months}} = £1.875\text{m}$$

Note 2: Employees not being used

Thirty-five workers are already employed by Relco plc but are not being used on any existing construction projects.

The salaries of these workers does not represent a relevant cost for the hotel project since the cost is a committed cost for Relco plc (assuming that these 35 workers were not about to be made redundant).

Relco plc will have to pay this cost whether they tender for the hotel project or not.

Note 3: Employees to be transferred from shopping centre project

The salaries of the 15 workers will have to be paid by Relco plc whether it tenders for the hotel project or not. So the salaries cost is not relevant to the decision. However, the penalty cost of £1.5 million is relevant. It would only be suffered if the hotel project were to go ahead and so must be covered by the tender price. Also, the additional labour costs of £300,000 associated with the shopping centre project are relevant for the same reason.

So relevant cost = £1.5m + £0.3m = £1.8m

Note 4: Materials

Materials for the hotel will cost £2.1 million less the 10% discount expected to be offered by suppliers.

Therefore, relevant cost is 90% × £2.1m = £1.89m

Note 5: Equipment already owned

The net book value of £500,000 is irrelevant, being made up of the original cost of the equipment (sunk) and less accumulated depreciation (non-cash).

The equipment has no other use at present but could be sold for £600,000. This amount would be foregone if the hotel project were to go ahead and is hence a relevant cost.

So relevant cost is £600,000.

Note 6: Equipment to be hired

This is an incremental (hence relevant) cost of:

18 months × £30,000 per month = £540,000

Note 7: Materials for roof

This is an incremental (hence relevant) cost, and at today's exchange rate the cost is:

$$\frac{€600,000}{€1.40} = £428,571$$

(b) Other factors that should be taken into account would include:

Exchange rate £:€

If it is expected that the £:€ exchange rate may move against the company, an estimate should be made of the roof materials cost using a forecast exchange rate.

It would be useful for a contract to be drawn up containing a clause specifying that the tender price is subject to alteration if the exchange rate changes beyond a certain amount of € per £1.

Competitor's tender prices

If possible, the likely tender price that competitors may submit for the contract should be considered. However, this information may be difficult to ascertain. Also it should be remembered that the lowest price tendered for a contract does not always result in the contract being awarded to the lowest cost bidder. Other factors such as reputation, quality, reliability and financial stability of the bidding companies are likely to be taken into consideration by the company awarding the contract.

Other opportunities

Other construction projects may exist that Relco plc could tender for, which might yield a larger potential mark-up than 35% and might possibly lead to further work as well.

Feasibility of 18-month timeframe

Before tendering, Relco plc must assess whether they feel that 18 months is a sufficiently long timeframe in order to complete the hotel construction work to the required specification. There might be hidden penalty clauses for over-running the 18-month time period which have not been brought to Relco plc's attention.

4.13 (a) There are a number of things wrong with Jim Elliott's statement. They are

1 The statement contains mixed-up thinking, which does not compare like with like. It consists of a mix of "relevant costs saved", but not all these costs are saved, and compares this with the additional total cost.

2 If the statement is an attempt to assess the proposal, it should include more than the next year's figures. This is because next year's figures would not be typical because of the inclusion of redundancy costs, for example. Also, demand increases year by year and this should be taken into account by calculating increased revenue and opportunity costs on cost of sales and so on.

3 There is no attempt to include the gain from selling more sensors. The additional cost per SCB is calculated incorrectly: it should be based on bought-in price less marginal cost (£116 − £88). This should then be multiplied by 58,000 units and the directly attributable fixed costs of £250,000 deducted from the total.

4 Assuming the costs under "saving in" are intended to be relevant.

5 The purchasing officer's salary should not be included as it must be assumed that she will still be employed to do the other half of her work and will receive a full salary.

6 Cost of placing an order would normally include the salary cost of the purchasing officer and so Jim's figure seems to be incorrect as the purchasing officer's salary has been dealt with separately.

7 The new liaison officer's salary is omitted.

8 Sixteen members of the production team still appear to be employed – we are not told whether they are transferred to other departments and so cannot judge what should be done with this cost. However, it should probably be included as a saving with the other 72, on the basis that they must be going to do a useful job elsewhere in the factory.

9 No redundancy costs are included: these are 72 staff × £4,000 = £288,000.

10 Costs for transportation of materials are included. These would normally be included in the direct material cost, which has been brought into the "additional cost calculation per SCB" and so should not be included here as a separate item.

(b)   *Note*: There are a number of different ways of answering this question.

	Year 2002/03	Year 2003/04	Year 2004/05	Total
CURRENT POSITION – Units	58,000	60,500	60,500	
	£'000	£'000	£'000	£'000
Additional business £400 × 3,000 units, etc.	1,200	2,200	2,200	
Variable cost £75 × 3,000 units, etc.	(225)	(412.5)	(412.5)	
Fixed costs – SCBs		(130)	(130)	
— sensors		(300)	(300)	
	975	1,357.5	1,357.5	3,690
EXPAND PRODUCTION – Units	58,000	62,000	65,000	
	£'000	£'000	£'000	£'000
Additional business:				
2002/03 1,200				
2003/04 – 7,000 units × £400		2,800		
2004/05 – 10,000 units × £400			4,000	
CIF differential	(1,624)	(1,736)	(1,820)	
£116 − £88 = £28 × 58,000 units, etc.				
Additional costs:				
Inventory	(10)	(10)	(10)	
Redundancy	(288)			
Liaison officer	(30)	(30)	(30)	
Fixed costs – SCBs – cost saved	250	250	250	
— sensors		(300)	(500)	
	(502)	974	1,890	2,362
RENTAL OPTION – Units	58,000	60,500	60,500	
	£'000	£'000	£'000	£'000
Rent received 240 × 120 = 28,800 sq.m × £45	–	1,296	1,296	
Additional business	1,200	2,200	2,200	
CIF differential	(1,624)	(1,694)	(1,694)	
£116 − £88 = £28 × 58,000 units, etc.				
Additional costs:				
Stock	(10)	(10)	(10)	
Redundancy	(288)			
Liaison officer	(30)	(30)	(30)	
Fixed costs – SCBs – cost saved	250	250	250	
— sensors		(300)	(300)	
	(502)	1,712	1,712	2,922

(i) Using the time horizon in the question, it is better to continue producing SCBs and work overtime. The next best option is to buy in SCBs and rent out the space. Working overtime generates (£3,690 − £2,922 = £768,000) more profit over the three years than renting.

(ii) In the long term, there are a number of advantages in buying-in SCBs. These include:

Long-term overtime working is not good for quality production and this could affect sales in the long term.

The company may not be keen on turning down work due to lack of capacity as this may hinder the long-term development of the company.

If demand is sustained at 65,000 sensors or above in the long term, it is financially better to buy in SCBs and expand production. In 2004/05, sales of 65,000 units give a greater return over the overtime option of £532,500, but it would take another three years of production at this level to make it the best option in the long term. However, if production expanded to 68,000 units in year 2005/06 (a similar increase to that of previous years), the annual net gain over the overtime option would be £1,648,500 (see below). This is more than enough to make expansion the best option over a four-year assessment period.

	£
Additional business 13,000 units × £400	5,200
Less: CIF differential 68,000 units × £28	1,904
	3,296
Less: Other costs	290
	3,006

Against this, the main disadvantage is:

SCBs were developed and designed by the company; if they were bought-in, would this lead to a loss of skills? On the other hand, it does not appear that MOV plc can produce them profitably.

Overall, a decision on future capacity of the final product ought to be made separately from a decision on whether to buy-in a component. The company would be advised to try to solve its space problem by finding additional or alternative accommodation.

Linear
Programming

Linear Programming

5

Linear programming is a graphical decision-making tool to assist businesses in allocating several limited or scarce resources so as to achieve an objective: all of which sounds a bit grandiose!

If a business makes *two* products (this has to be the case for linear programming since we end up drawing a graph and a graph only has two axes – *x*-axis for one product and *y*-axis for the other product), and *finite* amounts of available *resources* and possibly other constraints on production as well, then linear programming can be used to determine how many units should be produced of each product.

We need to know what *objective* the business is striving to achieve, typically this will be to maximise profit or maximise revenue or possibly even minimise cost.

(The *simplex* technique can be used where a business makes more than two products.)

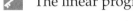 The linear programming technique involves six steps which are:

1 Define the variables.
2 Set up the objective function.
3 Set up the constraints.
4 Draw graph for the products, constraint lines and mark the feasible region.
5 Draw an example objective equation on the graph and move it outwards through the feasible region to determine the optimal product mix (move *outwards* if the business wants to *maximise* revenue or profit).
6 Conclude, that is, tell the business how many units of each product that it should produce in order to achieve its objective.

❓ Questions

5.1 A company employs skilled technicians and unskilled labourers. Skilled technicians must not be more than 40% of the total number of persons employed. If skilled technicians are denoted by *x* and unskilled labourers by *y*, which of the following inequalities expresses this constraint?

A $\dfrac{2x}{5} \leq x + y$

B $x \leq \dfrac{2(x + y)}{5}$

C $\dfrac{2x}{5} \leq y$

D $x \leq \dfrac{2y}{5}$

E $4x \leq x + y$

(3 marks)

5.2 There are several limitations associated with the simplex technique. Which of the following are limitations of the technique?

   (i)   All values used in the technique need to be estimated.
   (ii) The technique can only work for two products.
   (iii) The technique assumes linear relationships.
   (iv) Constraint equations can be difficult to formulate.

(2 marks)

5.3 A company makes four products and is subject to five constraints (including the non-negativity constraints). It has one objective function. How many slack variables will there be in a simplex model solution?

(2 marks)

5.4

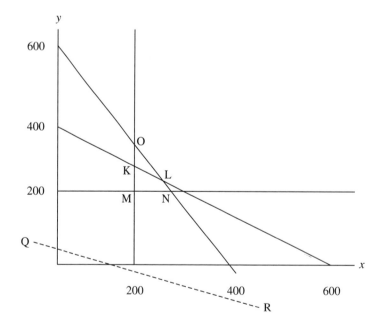

Line QR represents the objective function and the feasible region lies inside KLNM.

The objective of the business is to maximise profit.

At which point on the graph will the business have to produce in order to achieve its objective?

A Point K
B Point L
C Point M
D Point N
E Point O

(3 marks)

5.5 A company using linear programming wishes to determine how many units of its two products, J and N to produce. Annual production of product J will be j units and for product N it will be n units. A binding contract to supply 600 units of J to an existing customer has been signed and will apply for the forthcoming year. However, production of product N is subject to control by an industry regulator such that no more than 1,000 units can be produced in any one year.

Product J requires 90 minutes of labour time per unit. Product N requires 240 minutes of labour time per unit. The company believes that 250,000 hours of labour time will be available during the forthcoming year.

Identify the relevant constraints?

(3 marks)

5.6 A UK-based cycle manufacturer has decided to penetrate the Euro-zone by selling in Italy two bikes from its existing range. The two most popular bikes in terms of sales to the UK market are the "Trailraiser" and the "Coolspin".

A new factory is to be built in Italy to manufacture these two products for the Italian market (at a later date they may even be sold to other countries in the Euro-zone). Three processes are involved in making bikes and the amount of time available for each, given the expected number of machines to be purchased for each process, are as follows:

Process 1: Preparation of materials
Process 2: Construction
Process 3: Quality control and packaging.

Maximum machine time available during first year of operation:

Process 1: 36,000 hours
Process 2: 90,000 hours
Process 3: 22,500 hours

Bikes are made in batches, and spend the following amounts of time in the three separate processes:

	Trailraiser (hours)	Coolspin (hours)
Process 1	3	6
Process 2	15	12
Process 3	4.5	1.5

The expected selling prices and production costs of the two products are:

| | Trailraiser (per batch) | Coolspin (per batch) |
	€	€
Selling price	30.00	35.00
Variable production costs	20.00	23.00
Fixed production costs	4.00	8.00
Profit	6.00	4.00

The objective of the company is to maximise profit.

Requirement

Using the Linear Programming graphical technique, determine the optimal number of batches of each type of bike that should be made and sold to the Italian market.

(10 marks)

5.7 MF plc (IMPM 5/02 (Amended))

MF plc manufactures and sells two types of product to a number of customers. The company is currently preparing its budget for the year ending 31 December 2003 which it divides into 12 equal periods.

The cost and resource details for each of the company's product types are as follows:

| | Product type M | Product type F |
	£	£
Selling price per unit	200	210
Variable costs per unit:		
Direct material P (£2.50 per litre)	20	25
Direct material Q (£4.00 per litre)	40	20
Direct labour (£7.00 per hour)	28	35
Overhead (£4.00 per hour)	16	20
Fixed production cost per unit	40	50
	Units	*Units*
Maximum sales demand in Period 1	1,000	3,000

The fixed production cost per unit is based upon an absorption rate of £10 per direct labour hour and a total annual production activity of 180,000 direct labour hours. One-twelfth of the annual fixed production cost will be incurred in Period 1.

In addition to the above costs, non-production overhead costs are expected to be £57,750 in Period 1.

During Period 1, the availability of material P is expected to be limited to 31,250 litres. Other materials and sufficient direct labour are expected to be available to meet demand.

It is MF plc's policy not to hold inventory of finished goods.

Requirements

(a) Calculate the number of units of product types M and F that should be produced and sold in Period 1 in order to maximise profit.

(4 marks)

(b) Using your answer to (a) above, prepare a columnar budgeted profit statement for Period 1 in a marginal cost format.

(4 marks)

After presenting your statement to the budget management meeting, the production manager has advised you that in Period 1 the other resources will also be limited. The maximum resources available will be:

Material P	31,250 litres
Material Q	20,000 litres
Direct labour	17,500 hours

It has been agreed that these factors should be incorporated into a revised plan and that the objective should be to make as much profit as possible from the available resources.

(c) Use graphical linear programming to determine the revised production plan for Period 1. State clearly the number of units of product types M and F that are to be produced.

(10 marks)

(d) Using your answer to part (c) above, calculate the profit that will be earned from the revised plan.

(3 marks)

(e) Calculate and briefly explain the meaning of the shadow price for material Q.

(4 marks)

(Total = 25 marks)

5.8   W plc (IMPM 11/03)

W plc provides two cleaning services for staff uniforms to hotels and similar businesses. One of the services is a laundry service and the other is a dry-cleaning service. Both of the services use the same resources, but in different quantities. Details of the expected resource requirements, revenues and costs of each service are shown below:

	Laundry *$ per service*	*Dry-cleaning* *$ per service*
Selling price	7.00	12.00
Cleaning materials ($10.00 per litre)	2.00	3.00
Direct labour ($6.00 per hour)	1.20	2.00
Variable machine cost ($3.00 per hour)	0.50	1.50
Fixed costs*	1.15	2.25
Profit	2.15	3.25

* The fixed costs per service were based on meeting the budget demand for December 2003.

W plc has already prepared its budget for December based on sales and operational activities of 8,000 laundry services and 10,500 dry-cleaning services, but it is now revising its plans because of forecast resource problems.

The maximum resources expected to be available in December 2003 are

Cleaning materials	5,000 litres
Direct labour hours	6,000 hours
Machine hours	5,000 hours

W plc has one particular contract which it entered into six months ago with a local hotel to guarantee 1,200 laundry services and 2,000 dry-cleaning services every month. If W plc does not honour this contract it has to pay substantial financial penalties to the local hotel.

Requirements

(a) Calculate the mix of services that should be provided by W plc so as to maximise its profit for December 2003.

(9 marks)

The Sales Director has reviewed the selling prices being used by W plc and has provided the following further information:

- if the price for laundry were to be reduced to $5.60 per service, this would increase the demand to 14,000 services
- if the price for dry-cleaning were to be increased to $13.20 per service, this would reduce the demand to 9,975 services.

(b) Assuming that such selling price changes would apply to all sales and that the resource limitations continue to apply, and that a graphical linear programming solution is to be used to maximise profit,

  (i) State the constraints and objective function.

(6 marks)

  (ii) Use a graphical linear programming solution to advise W plc whether it should revise its selling prices.

(10 marks)
(Total = 25 marks)

 Answers

5.1 **B**

Total employees will be $x + y$

Number of skilled technicians is x

Number of technicians cannot be more than (and so must be less than or at most equal to) 2/5 (i.e. 40%) of the total number of employees.

Therefore, the inequality must be

$$x \le \frac{2(x + y)}{5}$$

5.2 (i)   A practical limitation is that selling price, costs and resource requirements have to be estimated for the products involved.

(ii) This is *not* a limitation of the technique. It is a *characteristic* of linear programming that the technique can only be used for a two product company. Remember that simplex technique can be used in the situation of multi-product companies.

(iii) This is a limitation. For example, if a company increases the volume of sales, it may have to offer discounts to selected customers which will have a downward effect upon contribution per unit and hence on the optimal solution. Similarly, as greater volumes are produced it may be possible for the company to achieve quantity discounts on the cost of materials purchased which would also have an effect upon contribution per unit.

(iv) Given that students and others attempting to set up a linear programming problem find the constraints challenging, this limitation should be self-evident.

5.3 In the simplex model technique, each constraint (other than the non-negativity constraints) requires a slack variable in the initial tableau.

Since there are three such constraints the answer is three.

5.4 **A**

The objective line QR must be pushed outwards as far possible – the more units that can be manufactured of each product on the *x*-axis and the *y*-axis, the more profit will be made.

Pushing the line QR outwards into the feasible region, it can be pushed through Points M, N and L and as far as Point K until it can be pushed no further. Point K is therefore the optimal point.

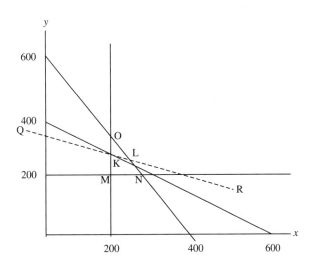

5.5   At least 600 units of product J must be produced to meet the terms of the recently signed contract. Of course the company may produce more than 600 units in order to supply other customers as well.

So, $j \geq 600$

At most 1,000 units of product N can be produced as a result of control by the industry regulator.

So, $n \leq 1,000$

As regards labour hours, at most 250,000 hours are expected to be available. Although product J requires 90 minutes of labour time per unit and product N requires 240 minutes of labour time per unit, these requirements must be converted into hours. So 1.5 hours is required per unit of product J and 4 hours is required per unit of product N.

So the labour hours constraint will be

$1.5j + 4n \leq 250,000$.

5.6

 Topic being tested

Linear programming as a technique to determine how many batches of two products (bikes in this case) should be produced in order to maximise profits for a cycle manufacturing business.

Approach

Use the following linear programming steps:

1   Define the variables.
2   Set up the objective function.
3   Set up the constraints.
4   Draw graph for the products, constraint lines and mark the feasible region.
5   Draw example objective equation on graph and move outwards through the feasible region to determine the optimal product mix.
6   Conclude, that is, tell the company how many batches of each type of bike it should produce in order to maximise profit.

Solution

The solution will be found using the linear programming steps as follows:

Step 1   Define the variables

Let x = number of batches of "Trailraiser" to be made.
Let y = number of batches of "Coolspin" to be made.

Step 2   Set up the objective function

The objective is to maximise profit.

For decision-making purposes we should consider *contribution* since fixed costs will be fixed irrespective of production volumes and the fixed cost per batch of each type of cake is subject to the apportionment technique used.

To maximise profit we must maximise contribution:

Contribution = $10x + 12y$

(Contribution per batch of "Trailraiser" = €30 − €20 = €10)
(Contribution per batch of "Coolspin" = €35 − €23 = €12)

Step 3   Set up constraints

There is a constraint equation for each process as well as the non-negativity constraint.

$3x + 6y \leq 36{,}000$	Process 1 constraint
$15x + 12y \leq 90{,}000$	Process 2 constraint
$4.5x + 1.5y \leq 22{,}500$	Process 3 constraint
$x \geq 0, y \geq 0$	Non-negativity constraints

To draw these on the graph we first plot the lines:

$3x + 6y = 36{,}000$	Process 1
$15x + 12y = 90{,}000$	Process 2
$4.5x + 1.5y = 22{,}500$	Process 3

$x = 0$
$y = 0$

To plot the line $3x + 6y = 36{,}000$
When $x = 0, y = 6{,}000$
When $y = 0, x = 12{,}000$

To plot the line $15x + 12y = 90{,}000$
When $x = 0, y = 7{,}500$
When $y = 0, x = 6{,}000$

To plot the line $4.5x + 1.5y = 22{,}500$
When $x = 0, y = 15{,}000$
When $y = 0, x = 5{,}000$

For an example objective line we could plot the line:

$10x + 12y = 60{,}000$

For this line
When $x = 0, y = 5{,}000$
When $y = 0, x = 6{,}000$

Note to student!!

Where did I get the 60,000 from?

Multiplying the numbers in front of x and y together gives $10 \times 12 = 120$

Multiplying by 1,000 since the other lines have values in the '000 gives $120 \times 1{,}000 = 120{,}000$.

I then looked at where this example objective equation would be if I plotted $10x + 12y = 120{,}000$ and it gave me a line out beyond the feasible region on the graph.

So I halved the value and found that plotting $10x + 12y = 60{,}000$.

This gave me a line in the feasible region which I could then move outwards through the feasible region to get to the optimal point.

Steps 4 and 5   Drawing the graph and example objective line

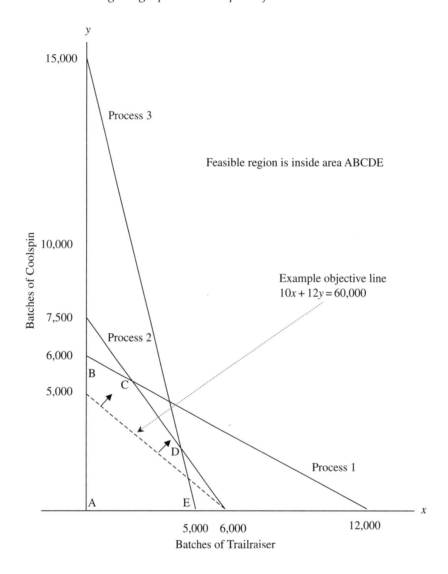

Pushing the example objective line outwards gives Point C as the optimal point. So we now need to find the values of x and y at Point C.

Point C is where the Process 1 and Process 2 lines cross.

That is, where

$3x + 6y = 36{,}000$

and

$15x + 12y = 90{,}000$

we can solve these using simultaneous equations.

Note to student!!

If you can not solve simultaneous equations or are running out of time in the exam, estimate the values of x and y at Point C by reading them off the graph.

$3x + 6y = 36,000$ Equation 1
$15x + 12y = 90,000$ Equation 2

To remove y:

$2 \times$ Equation 1 $-$ Equation 2

Gives

$6x + 12y = 72,000$
$\underline{15x + 12y = 90,000}$

$-9x \qquad\quad = -18,000$

So,
$x = 2,000$ batches of Trailraiser

Using Equation 1

Note to student!!

We could use Equation 1 or Equation 2 now to get the value of y knowing that the value of x is 2,000. It does not matter which equation we use since using either will give the same answer!

$3x + 6y = 36,000$ Equation 1
$3 \times 2,000 + 6y = 36,000$
$6,000 + 6y = 36,000$
$6y = 30,000$

So,
$y = 5,000$ batches of Coolspin.

Step 6   Conclusion

To maximise contribution and so maximise profit, the company should produce 2,000 batches of Trailraiser (Product X) and 5,000 batches of Coolspin (Product Y) in the Italian market.

5.7

(a)   *Product type*

	M	F
Contribution per product unit (£)	96	110
Material P per unit (litre)	8	10
Contribution per litre of material P (£)	12	11
Ranking	1st	2nd
Production/sales units	**1,000**	**2,325**
Material P used (litre)	8,000	23,250

(b) Budgeted profit statement for Period 1

	Product M £'000	Product F £'000	Total £'000
Sales	200	488.250	688.250
Variable costs:			
Direct material P	20	58.125	78.125
Direct material Q	40	46.500	86.500
Direct labour	28	81.375	109.375
Overhead	16	46.500	62.500
	104	232.500	336.500
Contribution	**96**	**255.750**	**351.750**
Fixed costs:			
Production			150.000
Non-production			57.750
			207.750
Profit			144.000

Let M be the number of product type M produced and sold.

The iso-contribution line is 96M + 110F (objective function).

The following lines are required for the graph:

$M \leq 1{,}000$ (maximum demand for M)
$F \leq 3{,}000$ (maximum demand for F)
$8M + 10F \leq 31{,}250$ (material P)
$10M + 5F \leq 20{,}000$ (material Q)
$4M + 5F \leq 17{,}500$ (direct labour)

Graph to show profit-maximising production plan.

The solution is that production/sales should be:

M   729 units
F   2,542 units

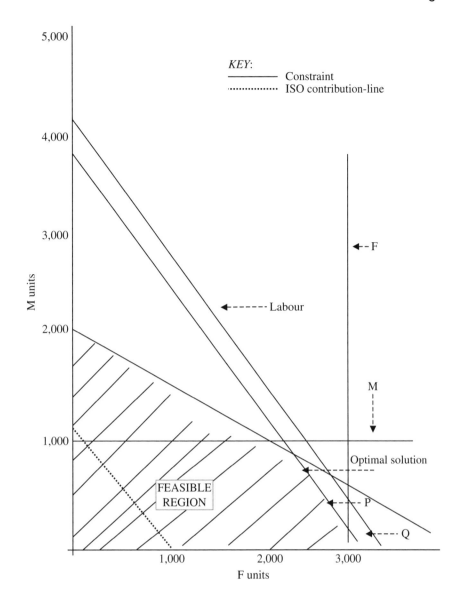

(d) The profit from the revised plan is as follows:

$£$

Contribution:

	£
729M × £96	69,984
2,542F × £110	279,620
	349,604

Less Fixed costs:

Production	150,000
Non-production	57,750
	207,750
Profit	141,854

(e) There are two constraints that are binding in respect of this revised solution. These are the availability of material P and material Q.

Material P availability was the limiting factor in requirement (a), so the effect of the limited availability of material Q can be measured by comparing the two profit values. There is a reduction in profit of £2,146 as a result of the scarcity of material Q, so this is the shadow price of the extra material Q required (1,625 litres) to return to the original solution from requirement (a).

5.8

(a) Resources required for budgeted activities:

Cleaning materials
(8,000L × 0.2 litre) + (10,500DC × 0.3 litre)   4,750 litres

Direct labour
(8,000L × 0.2 hour) + (10,500DC × 0.33 hour)   5,065 hours

Machine hours
(8,000L × 0.166 hour) + (10,500DC × 0.5 hour)   6,578 hours

Machine hours are the limiting factor

	Laundry	*Dry-cleaning*
Contribution per service unit	£3.30	£5.50
Machine hours per service unit	0.166	0.5
Contribution per machine hour	£19.80	£11.00
Ranking	1st	2nd
Minimum demand	1,200	2,000
Uses (machine hours)	200	1,000
Balance	6,800	5,334
Uses (machine hours)	1,133	2,667
Product mix (units)	8,000	7,334

(b)

Examiner's note: The following proof of the need to use a linear programming solution is included to assist students.

Revised maximum demand levels:

Laundry   14,000
Dry-cleaning   9,975

Revised resource requirements:

Cleaning materials
(14,000L × 0.2 litre) + (9,975DC × 0.3 litre)   5,792.5 litres

Direct labour
(14,000L × 0.2 hour) + (9,975DC × 0.33 hour)   6,091.75 hours

Machine hours
(14,000L × 0.166 hour) + (9,975DC × 0.5 hour)   7,311.5 hours

All resources are now binding – use linear programming to solve

(i)   Constraints (L = Laundry, DC = Dry-cleaning):

$$0.2L + 0.3DC \leq 5,000$$
$$0.2L + 0.33DC \leq 6,000$$
$$0.166L + 0.5DC \leq 5,000$$
$$14,000 > L \geq 1,200$$
$$9,975 > DC \geq 2,000$$

Objective function: Maximise $1.9L + 6.7DC = C$

(ii) The graphical linear programming solution (see graph below) yields:

	£
9,600DC units × £6.70 contribution per unit	64,320
1,200L units × £1.90 contribution per unit	2,280
Total contribution	66,600

Compared to:

	£
7,334DC units × £5.50 contribution per unit	40,337
8,000L units × £3.30 contribution per unit	26,400
Total contribution	66,737

Thus it appears that the new strategy should not be adopted, as it reduces contribution. However, as the difference is so small, further market research should be carried out.

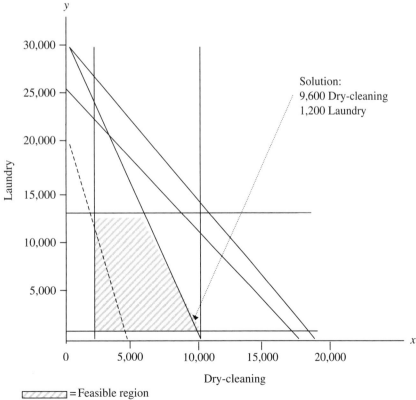

Graphical linear programming solution

Solution:
9,600 Dry-cleaning
1,200 Laundry

(y-axis: Laundry; x-axis: Dry-cleaning)

⬛⬛⬛ = Feasible region
───── = Constraint
- - - - - = Objective function (ISO – Contribution line)

Pricing

Pricing

6

Businesses must consider many *practical* factors before they can decide upon the eventual selling price of their product or service.

These should include:

- Product cost
- Competitor's prices
- What customers are prepared to pay
- Price of other products in the range, for example, complementary and substitute products
- Elasticity of demand
- Where the product is in the product life cycle
- The company objective, for example, profit maximisation or revenue maximisation
- Whether or not to offer incentives such as discounts
- The degree of product differentiation.

You need to be able to discuss these practical issues.

You must also be able to discuss the following:

- Penetration pricing
- Premium pricing
- Market skimming
- Loss leader pricing
- Product bundling.

π The company may have a *theoretical* objective such as to maximise profit or maximise revenue.

To maximise *profit* the company should produce and sell at a price where,

MC = MR (i.e. Marginal Cost = Marginal Revenue).

To maximise *revenue* the company should produce and sell at a price where,

MR = 0 (i.e. Marginal Revenue equals zero).

? Questions

6.1 The following information relates to a management consultancy:

Wage cost per consultant hour (senior consultant) £45.00
Wage cost per consultant hour (junior consultant) £26.00
Overhead absorption rate per consultant hour £20.50

The firm adds a 25% mark-up on marginal cost to arrive at the price to charge clients.

For client "Greenstart" 75 hours of senior consultant time and 30 hours of junior consultant time have been incurred. All staff are paid on an hourly basis.

What price should be charged to Greenstart?

(2 marks)

6.2 When deciding upon the price of a product which of the following items would not be taken into consideration?

A Cost of making the product.
B Price elasticity of demand.
C Cost of making other unrelated products.
D Prices charged by competitors serving the same market segments.
E Level of customer disposable wealth.

(2 marks)

6.3 When is market skimming pricing appropriate?

A If demand is very elastic.
B If the product is new and different.
C If there is little chance of achieving economies of scale.
D If demand is inelastic.
E If there is little competition and high barriers to entry.

(2 marks)

6.4 Which of the following is a recognised method of arriving at the selling price for the products of a business?

 (i)   Life cycle pricing
 (ii) Price skimming
(iii) Penetration pricing
(iv) Target costing

A (i) and (ii) only
B (i), (ii) and (iii) only
C (ii) and (iii) only
D (i), (iii) and (iv) only
E (i), (ii), (iii) and (iv)

(2 marks)

6.5 Maltov has established the following cost and revenue functions for the single product that it manufactures:

Price = £120 − 0.5 × quantity
Marginal revenue = £120 − 1 × quantity
Total cost = £250,000 + 20 × quantity

What price should Maltov charge for its product in order to maximise profit?

(2 marks)

6.6 The variable cost for product Alpha is £40 per unit. Budgeted sales are expected to be 8,000 units during the forthcoming year, and fixed costs are expected to be £30,000. If 8,000 units are sold the profit is expected to be £60,000.

What is the profit margin for product Alpha?

(2 marks)

6.7 The trust in charge of national landmarks offers discounted entry to visitors with a valid student identity card.

This price discrimination policy is on the basis of

A   Place
B   Usage
C   Market segment
D   Time
E   Product type

(2 marks)

Use the following information to answer the next two questions.

H is launching a new product which it expects to incur a variable cost of $14 per unit. The company has completed some market research to try to determine the optimum selling price with the following results. If the price charged was to be $25 per unit then the demand would be 1,000 units each period. For every $1 increase in the selling price, demand would reduce by 100 units each period. For every $1 reduction in the selling price, the demand would increase by 100 units each period.

Note: If Price (P) = a – bx; then Marginal Revenue = a − 2bx

6.8 Determine the selling price per unit needed to maximise profit.

(3 marks)

6.9 If the selling price was set to maximise *revenue*, what would be the resulting?

A   £6,125
B   £1,500
C   £4,625
D   £7,625
E   £1,750

(3 marks)

6.10 Market research by Company A has revealed that the maximum demand for product R is 50,000 units each year and that demand will reduce by 50 units for every £1 that the selling price is increased. Based on this information, Company A has calculated that the profit-maximising level of sales for product R for the coming year is 35,000 units.

Determine the selling price of each of the units at the profit-maximising level of sales.

(2 marks)

6.11 "Samsinging Ltd." is about to launch a new product to the UK market, the new product is called the "Songtime". Sales demand has been estimated based on product launches in a range of similar countries and the expected demand is to be between a low of 50,000 units per month and a high of 400,000 units per month depending upon the price ultimately charged.

The marketing department believe that 50,000 units would be sold if the price is set at £400 per unit. They have also advised that for every decrease in price of £12.50 per unit, an additional 25,000 units would be sold.

Fixed costs are expected to be £48 million per annum if the company produces 250,000 units or less. However, if the level of production exceeds 250,000 units, annual fixed costs are expected to increase by £6 million.

If 250,000 units or less are made, the variable production cost per unit is expected to be £240 per unit. If more than 250,000 units are made, the variable production cost per unit is expected to be £210 per unit. Variable selling cost per unit is expected to be £35 per unit if 150,000 units or less are sold, and £40 per unit if more than 150,000 units are sold.

Requirements

(a) Advise the company as to the price that should be set given that their primary objective is to maximise profit. Produce a table but consider only production and sales levels of 50,000 units, 100,000 units, 150,000 units, 200,000 units, 250,000 units, 300,000 units, 350,000 units and 400,000 units.

(5 marks)

(b) Briefly explain what is meant by market skimming, penetration pricing and market segmentation in the context of product pricing.

(3 marks)

(c) Briefly discuss the typical issues that a company should consider when setting selling prices for a new product about to be launched.

(2 marks)
(Total = 10 marks)

6.12 Staly plc has two wholly owned UK-based subsidiaries.

One of these subsidiaries, Brompton Ltd, manufactures plastic toys which it sells to toy retailers. Brompton Ltd is about to launch a new product but is unsure what price to charge. A firm of consultants have estimated the level of demand at several different prices. This information is as follows:

Price (£)	5	10	15	20	25	30	35	40
Level of demand in forthcoming year ('000 of units)	200	180	160	135	120	100	75	50

The cost of manufacturing the new toy has been estimated as follows:

	£ per unit
Direct materials	2.00
Direct labour	1.50
Variable overheads	2.50
	6.00

Fixed costs associated with manufacturing the new toy are expected to be £400,000 per annum. However, if production and sales exceed 150,000 units fixed costs are expected to increase by £50,000.

The second subsidiary, Electrics Ltd, assembles desktop computers using components sourced from suppliers of keyboards, microchips, monitors, speakers and so on. It sells these computers under its own brand name through 150 of its own outlets in major shopping centres throughout the UK.

It is to commence selling a new computer aimed at students. The management of Electrics Ltd believe that the price and marginal revenue equations are as follows:

Price equation:
$P = 2{,}000 - 0.01Q$

where P is selling price and Q is sales quantity in units.

Marginal revenue (MR) equation:
$MR = 2{,}000 - 0.02Q$

The cost of manufacture is expected to be:

	£ per unit
Direct materials (bought-in components)	400
Direct labour (assembly)	150
Variable overheads	50
Fixed overheads (apportioned)	200
	800

Requirements

(a) For Brompton Ltd, determine the price that should be set for the new toy in order to maximise profit for Brompton Ltd.

(4 marks)

(b) For Electrics Ltd, determine the price that should be set for the new computer under two circumstances:

to maximise profit for Electrics Ltd
to maximise revenue for Electrics Ltd.

(6 marks)
(Total = 10 marks)

6.13 R Ltd (IDEC 5/03 (Amended))

Just over two years ago, R Ltd was the first company to produce a specific "off-the-shelf" accounting software packages. The pricing strategy, decided on by the Managing Director, for the packages was to add a 50% mark-up to the budgeted full cost of the packages. The company achieved and maintained a significant market share and high profits for the first two years.

Budgeted information for the current year (Year 3) was as follows:

Production and sales	15,000 packages
Full cost	£400 per package

At a recent board meeting, the Finance Director reported that although costs were in line with the budget for the current year, profits were declining. He explained that the full cost included £80 for fixed overheads. This figure had been calculated by using an overhead absorption rate based on labour hours and the budgeted level of production which, he pointed out, was much lower than the current capacity of 25,000 packages.

The Marketing Director stated that competitors were beginning to increase their market share. He also reported the results of a recent competitor analysis which showed that when R Ltd announced its prices for the current year, the competitors responded by undercutting them by 15%. Consequently, he commissioned an investigation of the market. He informed the Board that the market research showed that at a price of £750 there would be no demand for the packages but for every £10 reduction in price the demand would increase by 1,000 packages.

The Managing Director appeared to be unconcerned about the loss of market share and argued that profits could be restored to their former level by increasing the mark-up.

Note: If price = $a - bx$ then marginal revenue = $a - 2bx$

Requirements

(a) Discuss the Managing Director's pricing strategy in the circumstances described above. Your appraisal must include a discussion of the alternative strategies that could have been implemented at the launch of the packages.

(10 marks)

(b) (i) Based on the data supplied by the market research, calculate the maximum annual profit that can be earned from the sale of the packages from Year 3 onwards.

(7 marks)

(ii) A German computer software distribution company, L, which is interested in becoming the sole distributor of the accounting software packages has now approached R Ltd. It has offered to purchase 25,000 accounting packages per annum at a fixed price of €930 per package. If R Ltd were to sell the packages to L, then the variable costs would be £300 per package.

The current exchange rate is €1 = £0.60.

Requirement

Draw a diagram to illustrate the sensitivity of the proposal from the German company to changes in the exchange rate and then state and comment on the minimum exchange rate needed for the proposal to be worthwhile.

(8 marks)

(Total = 25 marks)

6.14 AVX Ltd (DM 5/06 (Amended))

AVX Plc assembles circuit boards for use by high-technology audio video companies. One particular board is the CB45. Due to the rapidly advancing technology in this field, AVX Plc is constantly being challenged to learn new techniques.

AVX Plc initially priced each batch of CB45 circuit boards on the basis of its standard cost of £960 plus a mark-up of 25%. Recently the company has noticed that, due to increasing competition, it is having difficulty maintaining its sales volume at this price.

The Finance Director has agreed that the long-run unit variable cost of the CB45 circuit board is £672.72 per batch. She has suggested that the price charged should be based on an analysis of market demand. She has discovered that at a price of £1,200 the demand is 16 batches per month, for every £20 reduction in selling price there is an increase in demand of 1 batch of CB45 circuit boards, and for every £20 increase in selling price there is a reduction in demand of 1 batch.

Requirement

(a) Calculate the profit-maximising selling price per batch using the data supplied by the Finance Director.

(8 marks)

Note: If Price (P) = a − bx then Marginal Revenue (MR) = a − 2bx

The Technical Director cannot understand why there is a need to change the selling price. He argues that this is a highly advanced technological product and that AVX Plc should not reduce its price as this reflects badly on the company. If anything is at fault, he argues, it is the use of Standard Costing and he has asked whether Target Costing should be used instead.

Requirement

(b) (i)   Explain the difference between standard costs and target costs;
     (ii) Explain the possible reasons why AVX Plc needs to re-consider its pricing policy now that the CB45 circuit board has been available in the market for six months.

(7 marks)
(Total = 15 marks)

Answers

6.1   £

Salary costs:

Senior consultant 75 hours × £45	3,375.00
Junior consultant 30 hours × £26	780.00
Marginal cost	4,155.00
Mark-up (25%)	1038.75
Price to charge client	5,193.75

6.2 **C**

All of the above should be taken into account except for the *cost* of making other unrelated products.

6.3 **B**

A   If demand is very elastic, high market share and a market presence could be achieved quickly by charging a low-penetration pricing.

B   Here market skimming would be more appropriate. A high price could be charged to the "opinion leaders" who want to be seen to have the new product and are prepared to pay a high price.

C   It is difficult to charge a low price for a product where there are few opportunities for economies of scale since cost per unit will still be high irrespective of production volume.

D   If demand is inelastic, charging a low price will not have a beneficial effect upon sales volume and profit.

E   If there is little competition and high barriers to entry, such as in the pharmaceutical industry, there is no incentive for companies to charge a low price.

6.4 **B**

At first inspection all four appear to be methods of arriving at selling price.

However, target costing is a method to arrive at the cost at which a product should be produced for having worked backwards from the price already set for the product.

It is a method to arrive at product cost not product selling price.

6.5 To maximise profit Maltov must produce where MC = MR

(MC is Marginal Cost, MR is Marginal Revenue)

MC = £20
MR = £120 − Q

So to maximise profit:
£20 = £120 − Q

Therefore,
Q = £100

To calculate the price that must be sold:
Price = £120 − 0.5 × quantity

So,
Price = £120 − 0.5 × £100 = £120 − £50 = £70

6.6   Profit margin = Profit/Sales × 100%

So we need to calculate profit per unit and selling price per unit.

Profit per unit = £60,000/8,000 units = £7.50 per unit

Selling price:

            Sales revenue = Variable costs + Fixed costs + Profit
                          = £40 × 8,000 units + £30,000 + £60,000
                          = £410,000

So, selling price per unit = £410,000/8,000 units = £51.25 per unit

Profit margin = £7.50/£51.25 × 100% = 14.6%

Alternatively,

            Profit margin = Profit/Sales × 100%
                          = £60,000/£410,000 × 100% = 14.6%

6.7 **C**

The trust is discriminating on the grounds of market segment (segmenting using occupation).

6.8   Marginal cost (MC) = $14

Price (P) = $35 − 0.01q

Marginal Revenue (MR) = $35 − 0.02q

So if MC = MR then:

14 = 35 − 0.02q

0.02q = 21

q = 1,050

Price = $35 − (0.01 × 1,050) = $24.50.

6.9   In order to maximise revenue, the business needs to produce the number on units where marginal revenue equals zero.

The marginal revenue as an equation is:
Marginal revenue = £35 − £0.02x

Putting marginal revenue equal to zero gives:
35 − 0.02x = 0

So,
35 = 0.02x
x = 35 ÷ 0.02 = 1,750

This is telling us that to maximise revenue, the company must produce 1,750 units.

To arrive at the selling price we use the selling price equation we calculated in the previous question.

Selling price = £35 − £0.01x = £35 − £0.01 × 1,750 = £35 − £17.50 = £17.50

At this selling price and volume of output profit would be

	£
Sales (17.5 × 1,750 units)	30,625
Variable costs (14 × 1,750 units)	(24,500)
Fixed costs	(1,500)
Profit	4,625

So profit is £4,625.

6.10 To solve this we have to derive an equation as follows:
P = price and let X = demand in units

Then

$50P = 50,000 − X$
$$P = \frac{50,000 − X}{50}$$
$P = 1,000 − 0.02X$

We are told that the profit maximising level of sales is 35,000 units.

So this is X.

Therefore,
$P = 1{,}000 - 0.02 \times 35{,}000 = 1{,}000 - 700 = £300$

6.11

 Topic being tested

Pricing policy

Approach

Part (a) – Arrive at a selling price by using a tabular approach for selected sales volumes and associated prices.

Part (b) – Discuss practical pricing methods and market segmentation using your learned knowledge.

Part (c) – Discuss typical factors to be considered when setting selling prices by doing a quick plan using common sense to generate ideas.

It is often advisable to attempt the written parts of questions of this style first if possible. Time pressure usually applies to numerical parts of questions more so than written parts.

Use short punchy paragraphs with spaces between them in all written answers.

Make it easy to mark!

Solution

(a) The price to set which will maximise profit for "Samsinging Ltd." can be found by using a table to calculate the profit resulting for the given price and related sales volumes.

Table for sales levels *per month*

Sales quantity ('000 units)	50	100	150	200	250	300	350	400
Price per unit (£)	400	375	350	325	300	275	250	225
Revenue (£m)	20	37.5	52.5	65	75	82.5	87.5	90
Variable production cost per unit (£)	240	240	240	240	240	210	210	210
Variable production costs (£m)	12	24	36	48	60	63	73.5	84
Fixed production costs (£m)	4	4	4	4	4	4.5	4.5	4.5
Variable selling cost per unit (£)	35	35	35	40	40	40	40	40
Variable selling costs (£m)	1.75	3.5	5.25	8	10	12	14	16
Profit (£m)	2.25	6.0	7.25	5.0	1.0	3.0	(4.5)	(14.5)

The maximum profit is £7.25 million if 150,000 units are sold at a price of £350 per unit.

So the company should set a selling price of £350 per unit.

(b) *Market skimming*

This is where a high price is initially charged for a new product. It will be aimed at the early adopters who are seen as being the "top of the market", hence the name market skimming – skimming off the "top" customers.

This pricing strategy would be appropriate for the launch of a high-technology product such as plasma screen televisions.

Penetration pricing

This is where the initial price of the new product is low in order to penetrate the market so as to achieve a market presence quickly and hopefully also achieve high market share.

It can be justified by economies of scale cutting product costs if the high market share is achieved.

This pricing strategy would be appropriate for the launch of a low-technology product such as a new chocolate bar.

Market segmentation

Market segmentation involves splitting or segmenting the "mass market" into different subgroups of customers.

Different products or services can then be designed and priced according to the different needs of customers in different segments. Similarly, promotional techniques can be used which focus on these customers.

For example, Porsche sell expensive sports cars to wealthy people at high prices whereas Proton sell relatively cheap cars to people with lower incomes or little interest in expensive cars.

(c) There are several typical issues that a company should consider when setting the selling price for a new product about to be launched. These would include:

- The likely price to be charged by competitors launching a similar new product.
- The price that "early adopters" are expected to be prepared to pay.
- The level of sales in unit terms that the company wishes to achieve in the short term.

The objective of the company:

- high market share, so a fairly low initial price to generate demand, that is, penetration pricing
- high profit per unit, so a high price and low market share, that is, market skimming.

6.12

> ⚠ *Topic being tested*
>
> Part (a) – Price setting using a tabular approach.
> Part (b) – Price setting using an equation approach.
>
> *Approach*
>
> Part (a) – Given that the price and volume of sales has been presented as a table it makes sense to calculate the profit for each piece and quantity combination also using a tabular approach and then select the price at which the level of profit is maximised.
> Part (b) – When equations are given, this should prompt you to remember that to maximise profit we must set MC = MR (Marginal Cost equal to Marginal Revenue), and to maximise revenue we must set MR = 0.

Solution

(a) Brompton Ltd wishes to determine the price at which the new toy should be sold in order to maximise profit. A tabular approach can be used as follows:

Price (£)	5	10	15	20	25	30	35	40
Quantity of units ('000)	200	180	160	135	120	100	75	50
Sales £'000	1,000	1,800	2,400	2,700	3,000	3,000	2,625	2,000
Variable costs (£6 × no. of units) £'000	1,200	1,080	960	810	720	600	450	300
Fixed costs £'000	450	450	450	400	400	400	400	400
Profit/(Loss)	(650)	270	990	1,490	1,880	2,000	1,775	1,300

Profit is maximised when the price is set at £30 per unit. This is therefore the price that should be set by Brompton Ltd.

(b) In order for Electrics Ltd to *maximise profit* it should produce where

$$MC = MR$$

Since Marginal Cost is the addition to cost of making one more unit, this will be the total *variable* cost of £600 per unit.

MR is given as

$$MR = 2,000 - 0.02Q$$

So setting MC = MR gives
$$600 = 2,000 - 0.02Q$$
$$2,000 - 600 = 0.02Q$$
$$1,400 = 0.02Q$$
$$1,400 \div 0.02 = Q$$

Therefore,
$$Q = 70,000 \text{ units}$$

So in order to maximise profit, Electrics Ltd should produce and sell 70,000 units per annum.

The selling price should be:
$P = 2,000 - 0.01Q$
$P = 2,000 - 0.01 \times 70,000 = 2,000 - 700 = £1,300$

So the selling price in order to maximise profit should be £1,300 per computer.

In order for Electrics Ltd to *maximise revenue* it should produce where

$MR = 0$

That is,
$2,000 - 0.02Q = 0$

So
$2,000 = 0.02Q$
$2,000/0.02 = Q$
$Q = 100,000$ units

At a price of:
$P = 2,000 - 0.01Q$
$P = 2,000 - 0.01 \times 100,000$
$P = 2,000 - 1,000 = £1,000$

In order to maximise revenue, Electrics Ltd should produce and sell 100,000 computers at a price of £1,000 per computer.

6.13

(a) Appraisal of the current pricing strategy

Managing Director's current pricing method

	£
Cost	400
50% mark-up	200
Selling price	600

Drawbacks

As can be seen, the cost-plus approach adds a mark-up to the cost to arrive at the selling price. There are many drawbacks associated with this pricing method as follows:

- It completely ignores the market, hence the reason why the selling price is out of line with competitors.
- It focuses entirely on internal costs.
- It ignores competitors' reactions which has resulted in the competitors reducing prices as soon as the company released theirs.
- It can result in different selling prices due to the different absorption methods used when determining the total cost.
- It ignores the distinction between incremental and fixed costs.
- It fails to ensure that the quantity produced will be sold since the company does not know if the price is in line with the customer's perceptions of the value of the product.

- It is based on the belief that demand for the software is inelastic, that is, an increase in price will not lead to any significant reduction in demand. If this were true then increasing prices would clearly lead to increased demand. However, this view is not supported by the market research information. Therefore, increasing prices are likely to lead to a fall in demand and hence fall in profitability.

Benefits

There are however, benefits to this method of pricing which include the following:

- It ensures that all costs are covered and a desired profit is achieved. So far this has been achieved with the pricing of the software packages, as they have been profitable to date.
- It is easy to calculate, as once cost is determined a simple mark-up on these costs identifies the selling price.
- It allows the delegation of the price setting to more junior finance staff.
- It allows the company to avoid the costs involved in seeking information about the level of demand in the market.
- It allows the maintenance of relatively stable prices and any price increases are easier to justify to clients.

Alternative pricing strategies

Price skimming

This method of pricing sets high initial prices in an attempt to exploit those sections of the market which are relatively insensitive to price changes. As R Ltd's product was the first of its type it could have initially set high prices to take advantage of the novelty appeal of a new product as demand would have been inelastic. If this approach had been used, R Ltd could have subsequently reduced the price to remain competitive in the market.

Penetration pricing

This method sets very low prices in the initial stages of a product's life cycle to gain rapid acceptance of the product and therefore a significant market share. If R Ltd had used this approach it could have discouraged entrants into the market.

Demand-based approach

With this method R Ltd could have utilised some market research information to determine the selling price and level of demand to maximise company profits. This method, however, does pose the following drawbacks:

- It is dependent on the quality of the market research information.
- It also assumes a competitive market; that is, the actions of competitors will not impact on actual demand for the software package.
- It is difficult to estimate the demand curve.
- It is difficult to incorporate the effect of competition.
- This method assumes that price is the only factor that influences the quantity demanded – other factors like quality, packaging, advertising, promotion, credit terms, after sales service are ignored.
- The marginal cost curve for our packages can only be determined after considerable analysis and the final results (£320) are only an approximation of the true marginal cost function.

However, this method does benefit from

- A useful insight that stresses the need for managers to think about price-demand relationships even if the relationship cannot be measured precisely.
- A consideration of the marketplace.
- Considering only incremental costs.

(b) (i) Optimum selling price and maximum annual profit

Optimum selling price and level of demand can be found when marginal cost equates to marginal revenue:

Demand	£750 − £0.01X
Marginal revenue	£750 − £0.02X
Marginal cost	£320
Marginal cost = marginal revenue	£320 = £750 − £0.02X
	X = 21,500
	Price = £750 − £10/1,000 (21,500) = £535

Revised profit		£
Selling price		535
Variable cost		320
Contribution per unit		215
Total contribution	£215 × 21,500	4,622,500
Less: Fixed costs		1,200,000
Profit		3,422,500

(ii) See diagram on next page.

Workings

Current contribution (b) (i)	£4,622,500

Contribution from exporting to L

((€930 × 0.60) − £300) × 25,000	£6,450,000

R Ltd should sell all of their output to L as it will increase contribution by £1,827,500.

However, if the exchange rate falls to €1 = £0.20 then negative contribution will be generated:

((€930 × 0.20) − £300) × 25,000	(£2,850,000)

Comment

As can been seen from the graph if the exchange rate falls to €1 = £0.52 (i.e. a 13.33% drop) then R Ltd will be indifferent as to whether they sell the accounting packages themselves or export them to L. If the exchange rate falls below €1 = £0.52, then R Ltd should sell the accounting packages themselves. R Ltd needs to assess the likelihood of the Euro falling in value.

Exporting to L = £6,450,000 in contribution at an exchange rate of 60p

Selling themselves = £4,622,500 in contribution at an exchange rate of 52p

Negative point = £2,850,000 in contribution at an exchange rate of 20p.

Sensitivity graph

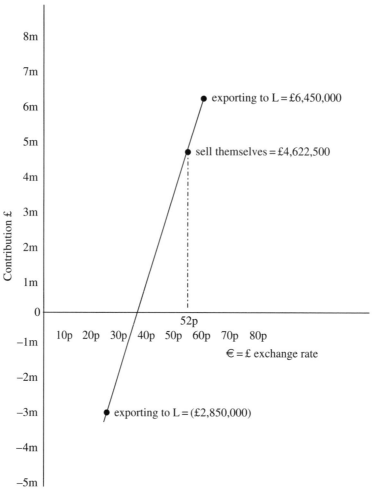

6.14

(a) The marginal cost and selling price per batch are as follows:

Marginal cost = £672.72

Demand at price of £1,200 = 16 batches and demand increases by 1 unit for every £20 reduction in selling price.

Therefore, Price = £1,520 − 20q

Marginal Revenue = £1,520 − 40q

Equating marginal cost and marginal revenue:

672.72 = 1,520 − 40q

40q = 847.28

q = 21.182

Price = £1,520 − (20 × 21.182) = £1,096.36

(b)

(i) A standard cost is an expected cost based on a measurement of the resources required to deliver a unit of a product or service and the prices expected to be paid for each unit of the resource. It is used as part of a Standard Costing system to control the costs incurred by an organisation.

A target cost is a cost to be achieved by a series of changes so as to achieve a target profit. It is used as part of Target Costing – a technique that identifies the market price of a product or service and determines the target cost to be achieved in order to earn a target profit.

Thus a target cost is driven by an external market price which is not controllable by the organisation whereas a standard cost is an internal control mechanism.

(ii) Now that the product has been in the marketplace for six months it is no longer unique as competitors have been able to purchase the product and reverse engineer it to determine how it works. As a consequence AVX Plc is probably facing competition and hence its difficulty in selling the circuit boards for £1,200 per batch. AVX Plc is no longer able to set its own prices without regard for the actions of its competitors; as a result they have to accept the market price.

The Value Chain – TQM

The Value Chain – TQM

7

A number of changes to management approach have developed in recent years. You must make sure that you understand the ideas that drive them, as well as the consequences for management decisions.

 JIT (just in time)

Producing items for immediate despatch to customer rather than for stock.

Often referred to as "demand-pull" production: demand from the customer activates the process.

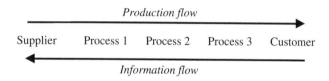

Production flow

Supplier   Process 1   Process 2   Process 3   Customer

Information flow

Decisions are based around customer demand, low stocks and quality issues.

 TQM (total quality management)

Aim is to continuously improve quality.
Quality is as defined by the customer.
A company should avoid defects rather than correct them.

Costs are categorised into four headings:

Prevention costs
Ensuring failures do not happen, for example, staff training, better quality materials.
Appraisal costs
Checking for failures, for example, quality testing, discarding tested items.
Internal failure costs
Cost of defects discovered in the company, for example, repair costs, scrapping costs.
External failure costs
Cost of defects discovered by the customer, for example, replacement cost, loss of
    goodwill.

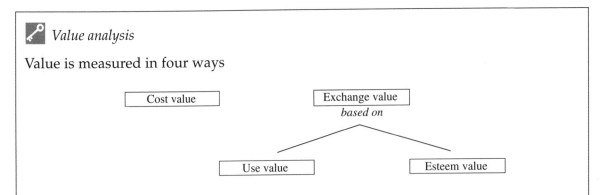

Value analysis

Value is measured in four ways

Cost value is the production cost.
Exchange value is the value to the customer (potential selling price).
Use value is the benefit the customer gets from consuming the product.
Esteem value is the prestige (and similar) that the client gets from association with the product.

A company should seek to boost exchange value and/or reduce cost value – it does this by eliminating non-value adding activities.

❓ Questions

7.1 The following statements have all been claimed to relate to the adoption of a TQM approach.

(i) Employees should focus on the requirements of their customers, both internal and external.
(ii) Standard costing is unlikely to be used as a method of control.
(iii) TQM companies often dispense with the quality control department.

Which of these statements are substantially true?

(2 marks)

7.2 Which of the following costs are likely to be reduced on the introduction of a JIT system in a company?

(i) Purchasing costs
(ii) Inventoryholding costs
(iii) Ordering costs
(iv) Information system costs

(2 marks)

7.3 Which of the following statements relating to JIT and TQM approaches is most closely related to the truth?

A TQM and JIT are not very compatible approaches since their focus is different: one focuses on quality and the other on inventory levels.
B TQM and JIT are not usually seen together since TQM is used by service companies and JIT by manufacturing companies.
C TQM and JIT are very compatible approaches as they are both largely focused on customer satisfaction.
D TQM and JIT are not compatible approaches since TQM requires there to be inventory so that quality checking can take place.

(2 marks)

...ɪe following is not a term normally used in value analysis?

A   Resale value
B   Use value
C   Esteem value
D   Cost value

(2 marks)

7.5   Which of the following is not suitable for a JIT production system?

A   Batch production
B   Jobbing production
C   Process production
D   Service production

(2 marks)

7.6   Companies that embrace TQM often split their costs into four categories: prevention costs, appraisal costs, internal failure costs and external failure costs.

A company wants to categorise the following costs.

(i)   Training staff in the importance of quality.
(ii)   Replacing, from inventory, a defective item returned by a customer.
(iii) Scrapping an item deliberately tested to destruction.
(iv)   Losses on the sale of items identified as rejects.

Which categories best reflect the nature of the above costs?

	Prevention costs	Appraisal costs	Internal failure costs	External failure costs
A	(i)	(ii)	(iii)	(iv)
B	(i)	(iii)	(iv)	(ii)
C	(ii)	(iv)	(iii)	(i)
D	(iii)	(i)	(iv)	(ii)

(2 marks)

7.7   Financial Advisors (DM 5/06)

A firm of financial advisors has established itself by providing high-quality, personalised, financial strategy advice. The firm promotes itself by sponsoring local events, advertising, client newsletters, having a flexible attitude towards the times and locations of meetings with clients and seeking new and innovative ideas to discuss with its clients.

The senior manager of the firm has recently noticed that the firm's profitability has declined, with fewer clients being interested in the firm's new investment ideas. Indeed, many clients have admitted to not reading the firm's newsletters.

The senior manager seeks your help in restoring the firm's profitability to its former level and believes that the techniques of *Value Analysis* and *Functional Analysis* may be appropriate.

Requirements

(a)   Explain the meanings of, and the differences between, Value Analysis and Functional Analysis.

(4 marks)

(b) Briefly explain the series of steps that you would take to imp.. Analysis for this organisation.

(6 marks)

(Total = 10 marks)

7.8 AVN (DM 11/06)

AVN designs and assembles electronic devices to allow transmission of audio/ visual communications between the original source and various other locations within the same building. Many of these devices require a wired solution but the company is currently developing a wireless alternative. The company produces a number of different devices depending on the number of input sources and the number of output locations, but the technology used within each device is identical. AVN is constantly developing new devices which improve the quality of the audio/visual communications that are received at the output locations.

The Managing Director recently attended a conference on world class manufacturing entitled "The extension of the value chain to include suppliers and customers" and seeks your help.

Requirements

Explain

(i)   the components of the extended value chain; and

(ii) how each of the components may be applied by AVN. **(3 marks)**

(7 marks)

(Total = 10 marks)

7.9 MD (DM 5/06)

The Managing Director of a manufacturing company based in Eastern Europe has recently returned from a conference on modern manufacturing. One of the speakers at the conference presented a paper entitled "Compliance versus Conformance – the quality control issue". The Managing Director would like you to explain to her some of the concepts that she heard about at the conference.

Requirement

Prepare a report, addressed to the Managing Director, that discusses quality costs and their significance for the company. Your report should include examples of the different quality costs a nd their classification within a manufacturing environment.

(10 marks)

Note: 2 marks are available for report format

7.10 PG plc (IMPM 11/02)

PG plc manufactures gifts and souvenirs for both the tourist and commercial promotions markets. Many of the items are similar except that they are overprinted with different slogans, logos and colours for the different customers and markets. For many years, it has been PG plc's policy to produce the basic items in bulk and then overprint them as required, but this policy has now been questioned by the company's new Finance Director.

She has also questioned the current policy of purchasing raw materials in bulk from suppliers whenever the periodic inventory review system indicates that the re-order level has been reached.

She has said that it is most important in this modern environment to be as efficient as possible, and that bulk purchasing and production strategies are not necessarily the most efficient strategies to be adopted. She has suggested that the company must carefully consider its approaches to production, and the associated costs.

Requirements

(a) Compare and contrast the current strategies of PG plc for raw materials purchasing and production with those that would be associated with a JIT philosophy.

(15 marks)

(b) Explain what is meant by cost reduction.

(3 marks)

(c) Explain how PG plc might introduce a cost reduction programme without affecting its customers' perceptions of product values.

(7 marks)
(Total = 25 marks)

7.11 SG plc (IMPM 11/02)

SG plc is a long-established food manufacturer which produces semi-processed foods for fast-food outlets. While for a number of years it has recognised the need to produce good quality products for its customers, it does not have a formalised quality management programme.

A director of the company has recently returned from a conference, where one of the speakers introduced the concept of TQM and the need to recognise and classify quality costs.

Requirements

(a) Explain what is meant by TQM and use examples to show how it may be introduced into different areas of SG plc's food production business.

(12 marks)

(b) Explain why the adoption of TQM is particularly important within a JIT production environment.

(5 marks)

(c) Explain four quality cost classifications, using examples relevant to the business of SG plc.

(8 marks)
(Total = 25 marks)

☑ Answers

7.1　(i)　Since quality is customer defined, everyone should become customer focused.

(ii)　Standard costing implies that there is a standard that is good enough, TQM is based on continuous improvement.

(iii)　Quality control departments are believed to reinforce the idea that quality is someone else's problem, instead quality is incorporated into everyone's targets.

7.2　(i)　Purchasing costs will increase due to the extra requirements applied to suppliers.

(ii)　Inventoryholding costs will reduce due to lower inventory levels.

(iii)　Ordering costs will increase due to the greater specification required and the increased number of small deliveries.

(iv)　Information system costs will increase due to the more accurate scheduling tools required.

7.3　**C**

A　Unless there is a quality programme of some type, a company cannot afford to have low stocks in case defective items need to be replaced from inventory.

B　Whilst TQM can be used by service companies, it is also seen in manufacturing and other productive industries along with JIT.

C　This is closely related to truth; customer satisfaction as regards quality and delivery times.

D　A TQM system is more concerned with ensuring that errors do not occur in the first place. Any checking of items can be undertaken during the production process itself.

7.4　**A**

The resale value is normally referred to as the "exchange value".

7.5　**A**

A　Batch production uses inventory to supply customers whilst other products are being produced. Inventory is avoided in a JIT system.

B　Jobbing production makes products to customer order, ideal for JIT.

C　Process production produces continuous output, as long as the speed of production can be regulated this can be tailored to customer requirements.

D　Services are always produced just in time as they cannot be stored.

7.6　**B**

(i)　This should help to *prevent* further failures.

(ii)　This is the cost of a quality *failure discovered externally* (it has been returned).

(iii)　This represents *appraising* the current production.

(iv)　This is the cost of a quality *failure discovered internally*.

7.7　(a)　Value analysis is an examination of the factors affecting the cost of a product or service with the objective of achieving the specified purpose most economically at the required level of quality and reliability.

Functional analysis is an analysis of the relationships between product functions, the cost of their provision and their perceived value to the customer.

Value analysis is thus a form of cost reduction which is based upon investigating the processes involved in providing a product or service whereas functional analysis focuses on the value to the customer of each function of the product or service and from this determines whether it is necessary to reduce the cost of providing each function.

(b) There are a series of steps that the firm of financial advisors need to use to implement Value Analysis into the organisation:

1 The firm needs to identify the requirements of their clients so that they can ensure that the services they provide give value to their clients. It has been stated that many clients do not read the firm's newsletters, clearly then the newsletters have no value to these clients in their present form. Perhaps the newsletters should be abandoned and their cost saved; or perhaps the form or content of the newsletter could be changed to make it more valuable from a client perspective.

2 Once the firm has identified the services that are valued by their clients they can then consider alternative ways of providing those services. Each of these alternatives is then costed.

3 A choice is made between the alternatives.

4 Implement the changes.

5 Evaluate the effect of the changes to determine whether the expected benefits have arisen.

7.8 (a) The Extended Value Chain includes both internal and external factors, whereas the Value Chain includes only the internal factors. The value chain is the sequence of business factors that add value to the organisation's products and services and comprises the following:

R&D	**Design**	**Production**	**Marketing**	**Distribution**	**Customer Service**

The Extended Value Chain adds Suppliers to the left hand side and Customers to the right hand side and recognises the importance of the relationships that the organisation has with these external parties in the overall process of adding value.

(b) AVN is operating in a market that is constantly changing as a result of new technology being developed. As a consequence AVN needs to ensure that their organisation is as efficient and flexible as possible. By building a relationship with a small number of suppliers, AVN can benefit by being assured of receiving quality components without the need for excessive inspection of deliveries. This relationship also benefits the supplier as they are guaranteed continuity of demand and can plan to meet AVN's production schedules.

Each of the internal factors can be applied to AVN as follows:

R&D
The generation of, and experimentation with, ideas for new devices and processes;

Design
The detailed planning and engineering of devices and processes;

Production
The coordination and assembly of resources to produce a product;

Distribution
The mechanism by which AVN's products are delivered to their customers;

Customer Services
The support activities provided to customers before and after the devices are installed.

Customers are the other important external factor within the extended value chain. AVN must meet the demands of customers both present and future. In a highly competitive market such as that found today, it is essential that AVN understands the needs of its customers and seeks to organise itself to meet those needs in the most efficient and effective way possible if it is to survive.

7.9 REPORT

To: Managing Director

From: Management Accountant

Subject: Quality

Date: May 2006

Introduction
This report provides the basis for discussion at the company's next board meeting. It outlines the approaches to quality that may be adopted by the company, in particular the conflict between "Conformance" and "Non-Conformance" in terms of costs and the perceptions of our customers.

Quality Costs
There are two broad approaches to the quality issue which each have their own costs, some of which are easier to identify and measure than others.

Quality costs can be analysed into two categories:

1   Costs of conformance; and
2   Costs of non-conformance.

Costs of conformance are the costs that are incurred in order to try to ensure that the quality of the final products or services meets the customers' expectations. This category can be sub-analysed into two further groups:

1   Appraisal costs – which are the costs incurred in testing/measuring and checking the product or service to ensure that it meets the quality targets that have been set; examples include the operating costs of test equipment; and

2   Prevention costs – which are costs that are incurred in order to prevent poor quality products or services from being produced; examples include training costs and routine maintenance of production equipment.

Costs of non-conformance are the costs that arise as a consequence of failing to meet the quality target. This category can also be sub-analysed into two further groups:

1   Internal failure costs – which are costs of reworking and correcting items of poor quality that have been discovered prior to despatch to customers; and
2   External failure costs – which are costs associated with poor quality products or services being delivered to the customer such as the cost of customer complaints.

Significance of quality costs

In the modern environment, with increased levels of competition and increasingly demanding customers who expect the products and services being provided to them to be of the highest quality, an organisation is required to carefully consider its target market and the price/quality relationship that its customers will demand.

The decision to incur inspection and appraisal costs is often seen as an attempt to minimise the costs of failure as there is clearly a relationship between incurring conformance costs and avoiding non-conformance costs. It is necessary to determine the level of failure that would be acceptable to customers given the specific price/quality relationship referred to above.

It is possible to achieve 100% quality in respect of all items delivered to customers but this would require that every item would have to be checked individually prior to its despatch. Clearly this would be time-consuming and costly.

An alternative approach would be to test a sample of the items to be delivered to customers and rely on that sample being representative of the entire consignment. Clearly this would be less time-consuming and therefore less costly but there is an increased risk that one or more of the items delivered would not be of the appropriate quality, thus increasing non-conformance costs.

Conclusion
This report has provided a basis of discussion at our next board meeting.

7.10   (a)   Just in time is a relatively recent development in the way in which organisations operate within their "value chains", linking through from material acquisition to servicing the retail customer. The traditional manufacturing system is classified as a "push" system. This is where materials are acquired in bulk, benefiting from quantity discounts, and where production is decoupled from sales, mass production achieving economies of scale, and the marketing function being tasked with selling the goods which have been produced, generally for inventory in the first instance.

Should PG plc move to JIT, it would convert to a "pull" system. This would mean that it would only manufacture in response to a customer order, and only acquire materials in response to a requirement from manufacturing. Inventory would be minimised. Some raw material inventory may be held, but no finished items should be in inventory. PG plc would therefore need to improve the flexibility of its employees (by making them multi-skilled) and of its equipment (reducing set-up times) so that it could quickly and at minimal cost switch between products in response to customer demand. Material suppliers should ideally deliver in small quantities so that no inventory is held. Suppliers should be able to respond immediately to orders, for example, a quantity of labels if a customer order is received for that number of products. To achieve this, competitive quotations would not be requested for each supply, but a small number of approved suppliers would be maintained, with whom there would be a long-term relationship.

While the JIT approach may well improve quality, reduce inventory loss (due to obsolescence or deterioration), increase speed of response and improve employee motivation, it is not certain that costs would reduce. A formal cost comparison may well identify cost increases due to the loss, for example, of the economies of bulk purchase. Advocates of JIT would counter that a "tighter" value chain, a more highly trained workforce, quicker identification of production problems, a zero defect philosophy and therefore greater customer satisfaction will lead to more work being done, and therefore to increasing long-term profitability.

The JIT system makes costs more visible than hitherto, and therefore offers greater scope for cost reduction, even though the objective is not to compete on cost as a primary marketing attraction.

(b) Cost reduction is the reduction in output costs without affecting the customer's perception of the value of the output. The attributes of the output are as attractive as before, but the cost of production is lower.

(c) A first step in a cost reduction programme would be to identify the characteristics of the products which are valued by customers. Characteristics or attributes that are not valued (non-value adding) can be considered for elimination, whereas those that add value should be enhanced or retained, and ways sought of reducing their cost without affecting their attractiveness in the perception of the consumer. Indeed, some attributes may be enhanced, even if this means extra cost!

7.11 (a) Total quality management is a management philosophy which emphasises "getting things right first time". It is argued that the costs associated with this policy will be lower than those resulting from the need to rectify defects caused by quality failures.

SG plc, should it introduce TQM, would, for example:

- Improve staff training and retraining, both in the TQM philosophy and in the technical aspects of the job.
- Improve product design so that production is easier and less likely to result in defects.
- Reduce the amount of inspection that is undertaken. As quality increases so should the non-value adding inspection cost decrease.
- Improve the information system so that relevant and timely information is produced and distributed to appropriate personnel.
- With better training, less costs due to spillage or poor storage will be incurred. Better product design in containers may reduce shipping costs and breakages. As quality improves, inspections can be reduced from say

one batch per 50 to one batch per 500, with a goal of eventually eliminating them completely. Production employees should be provided with daily throughput figures, set up and changeover time statistics, forward order details and so on, so that they can manage their workloads better.

(b) Within a JIT environment there is no inventory of any quantity, so any quality problem is likely to (and is intended to) immediately affect output levels. Any quality problem is therefore very costly – and a feature of JIT is that it is seen to be costly. To enable the system to work efficiently, therefore, quality is paramount. If this were not the case then the adoption of a JIT system would almost inevitably cause the demise of the organisation as stoppages would multiply, costs would increase significantly, and customer commitments would not be met. JIT therefore is founded on a zero defects goal, which requires TQM.

(c) Four quality cost classifications are:

Prevention costs – Costs associated with preventing the output of products which fail to conform to the specifications. The cost of preventative maintenance on food mixers would be one of such costs.

Appraisal costs – Costs associated with ensuring that production meets standards. The cost of inspecting foodstuffs would be an appraisal cost, whether they are bought-in ingredients or completed foodstuffs.

Internal failure costs – Costs of materials or products that fail to meet specifications. Such costs might be the cost of foodstuffs disposed of due to undercooking, the cost of equipment breakdowns, and associated production stoppages.

External failure costs – Costs arising when poor quality products are delivered to customers. The cost of replacement foodstuffs, of handling customer complaints and possibly of damaged reputation and financial damages if, for example, food poisoning is a result.

8

Activity-based
Approaches

Activity-based Approaches

8

If long-term decisions need to be made, an absorption costing system is needed. The system must be accurate and as discussed in Chapter 2 total absorption costing is unlikely to produce the required accuracy.

Direct product profitability (DPP)

This technique is used to spread overheads in retail organisations. Product-related costs such as warehousing, transport, refrigeration and insurance are spread over units according to drivers such as size, distance travelled, days spent chilled, value, etc. These costs are then deducted from the selling price, in addition to the bought-in price, to give the direct product profit.

Benefits include

- better cost analysis
- better pricing decisions
- better management of store and warehouse space
- the rationalisation of product ranges
- better merchandising decisions.

Activity-based costing

This was covered in Chapter 2. It is particularly useful where

- production overheads are high in relation to direct costs
- there is a great diversity in the product range
- products use very different amounts of the overhead resources
- consumption of overhead resources is not primarily driven by volume.

Customer profitability analysis

Using activity-based costing to create customer profiles and identify the profitability of customer types.

Activity-based management

A management system which uses activity-based cost information, such as those described here, to ensure that customer needs are met using the minimum of resources.

Pareto analysis

Based on the observed phenomenon that 80% of the population's wealth is owned by 20% of the people, the principle can be observed in many business situations, such as the relationship between

- Contribution and revenue
- Customers and profit
- Inventory items and inventory value.

⁉ Questions

8.1 What is the difference between activity-based costing (ABC) and activity-based management (ABM)?

(2 marks)

8.2 A hotel has identified that the overall profit earned when providing a room to a weekend traveller is less than that earned on providing a room during the week. They therefore decide to alter their pricing structure to attract more weekday guests. From the following list, identify the techniques that appear to have been used in this decision.

- Activity-based costing
- Activity-based management
- Direct product profitability
- Strategic activity management
- Customer profitability analysis

(3 marks)

8.3 Distinguish between primary and support activities in a value chain.

(4 marks)

8.4 A bakery produces and sells a range of products. The following represents the results for the last month

Product	Contribution £ (000)
Brown loaves	67
Family-sized cakes	53
Filled rolls	26
Individual cakes	83
Pasties and pies	16
Plain rolls	42
White loaves	94

Prepare a Pareto chart of product contribution and comment on the results.

(15 marks)

8.5 Which changes in the modern business environment have led to the need for ABC to replace more traditional approaches?

(5 marks)

8.6 X plc manufactures three products in a modern manufacturing plant, using cell operations. Budgeted output for April 2009 was

Product R 1,800 units in 36 batches
Product S 1,000 units in 10 batches
Product T 1,000 units in 40 batches

The product details are as follows:

Product:	R	S	T
Standard labour hours per batch	25	30	15
Batch size (units)	50	100	25
Machine set-ups per batch	3	2	5
Power (kJ) per batch	1.4	1.7	0.8
Purchase orders per batch	5	3	7
Machine hours per batch	10	7.5	12.5

During April 2009, the actual output was

Product R 1,500 units in 30 batches
Product S 1,200 units in 12 batches
Product T 1,000 units in 40 batches

The following production overhead budgetary control statement has been prepared for April 2009 on the basis that the variable production overhead varies in relation to standard labour hours produced.

Production overhead budgetary control report April 2009

	Original budget	Flexed budget	Actual	Variances
Output (standard hours produced)	1,800	1,710	1,710	
	£'000	£'000	£'000	£'000
Power	1,250	1,220	1,295	75 (A)
Stores	1,850	1,800	1,915	115 (A)
Maintenance	2,100	2,020	2,100	80 (A)
Machinery cleaning	800	760	870	110 (A)
Indirect labour	1,460	1,387	1,510	123 (A)
	7,460	7,187	7,690	503 (A)

After the above report had been produced, investigations revealed that every one of the individual costs could be classified as wholly variable in relation to the appropriate cost drivers.

Requirements

(a) Explain the factors that should be considered when selecting a cost driver.

(4 marks)

(b) (i) Calculate the budgeted cost per driver for each of the overhead costs.

(10 marks)

(ii) Prepare a production overhead budgetary control report for April 2009 using an activity-based approach.

(6 marks)

(Total = 20 marks)

8.7 Having attended a CIMA course on activity-based costing (ABC) you decide to experiment by applying the principles to the four products currently made and sold by your company. Details of the four products and relevant information are given below for one period:

Product	A	B	C	D
Output in units	120	100	80	120
Costs per unit	£	£	£	£
Direct material	40	50	30	60
Direct labour	28	21	14	21
Machine hours (per unit)	4	3	2	3

The four products are similar and are usually produced in production runs of 20 units and sold in batches of 10 units.

The production overhead is currently absorbed by using a machine hour rate, and the total of the production overhead has been analysed as follows:

	£
Machine department costs (rent, business rates, depreciation and supervision)	10,430
Set-up costs	5,250
Stores receiving	3,600
Inspection/quality control	2,100
Material handling and dispatch	4,620

You have ascertained that the 'cost drivers' to be used are as listed below for the overhead costs shown:

Cost	Cost driver
Set-up costs	Number of production runs
Stores receiving	Requisitions raised
Inspection/quality control	Number of production runs
Materials handling and dispatch	Orders executed

The number of requisitions raised on the stores was 20 for each product and the number of orders executed was 42, each order being for a batch of 10 of a product.

Requirements

(a) Calculate the total costs for each product if all overhead costs are absorbed on a machine hour basis.

(10 marks)

(b) Calculate the total cost of each product, using activity-based costing.

(10 marks)

(c) Calculate and list the unit product costs from your figures in (a) and (b) above, to show the differences and comment briefly on any conclusions which may be drawn which could have pricing and profit implications.

(10 marks)

(Total = 30 marks)

✅ Answers

8.1 In its most basic form, ABC is simply a technique for allocating overheads to units to provide more accurate product costs. When companies use ABC information for cost management – i.e. to make cost savings or control spending, it can be said that they have moved beyond ABC to ABM. ABM then, is the use of activity-based costing techniques to improve the business by for example, reducing costs, or profiling and targeting customers.

8.2

- Activity-based costing – To find the overall cost of providing a room, the overheads must have been absorbed using appropriate cost drivers
- Activity-based management – The activity-based cost information has been used to make a business decision – this is an example of activity-based management
- Customer profitability analysis – The activity-based costing method has been used to identify the type of customer (weekend/weekday) that is the most profitable

Direct product profitability is used in retailing to find the profitability of a particular item for sale and strategic activity management is used to identify and eliminate non-value activities, and improve competitive advantage.

8.3 An organisation's main activities, are known as the primary activities and should add value to the product or service. These would include:

- Inward movement of raw materials
- Manufacture
- Marketing
- Distribution
- After-sales service

The support activities (which are potentially non-value adding) would include information database and structure and human resource management. These areas must be carefully managed to ensure that they are assist the primary activities in adding value.

8.4 First, the results are rearranged in descending order of contribution and a cumulative contribution figure calculated.

Product	Contribution £ (000)	Cumulative contribution £ (000)	Cumulative %
White loaves	94	94	25
Individual cakes	83	177	46
Brown loaves	67	244	64
Family-sized cakes	53	297	78
Plain rolls	42	339	89
Filled rolls	26	365	96
Pasties and pies	16	381	100
	381		

The cumulative data can now be used to produce the required Pareto chart showing product contribution:

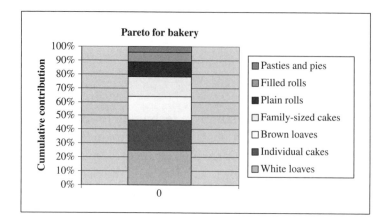

It is clear from the diagram that four of the product lines make up nearly 80% of the contribution for the bakery firm.

The most popular products are bread and cakes and with white loaves outselling all other products. Management attention should be focused on these areas.

8.5 Recent changes necessitating ABC include

- a proportionate increase in fixed costs making the sharing of them more significant
- the increase of flexibility and diversity, leading to extra costs associated with these factors
- increasing customer focus, leading to a wider variety of products
- increased competition, leading to the need for more realistic cost information
- the increased desire to control production systems, requiring information about what activities cause which costs.

8.6 (a) The main factor to be considered when selecting a cost driver should be that there is a cause and effect relationship between the cost driver and the costs. Such a relationship may exist because of

- physical relationship
- contractual arrangements
- implicit logic.

It is necessary to consider the correlation between the cost and the proposed cost driver, while recognising that they may both be influenced by a third, as yet unknown, factor.

(b) Each of the separate costs are assumed to be associated with cost drivers as follows:

Power	–	power per batch
Stores	–	purchase orders per batch
Maintenance	–	machine hours per batch
Machinery cleaning	–	machine set-ups per batch
Indirect labour	–	standard labour hours per unit

(i) Using the original budget data to set cost driver rates

Power

	kJ
R (1.4 kJ per batch × 36 batches)	50.4
S (1.7 kJ per batch × 10 batches)	17.0
T (0.8 kJ per batch × 40 batches)	32.0
	99.4

$$\text{Cost driver rate} = \frac{£1,250}{99.4 \text{ kJ}} = £12.5754/\text{kJ}$$

Stores

	Orders
R (5 orders per batch × 36 batches)	180
S (3 orders per batch × 10 batches)	30
T (7 orders per batch × 40 batches)	280
	490

$$\text{Cost driver rate} = \frac{£1,850}{490 \text{ orders}} = £3.7755 \text{ per purchase order}$$

Maintenance

	Machine hours
R (10.0 m/c hours per batch × 36 batches)	360
S (7.5 m/c hours per batch × 10 batches)	75
T (12.5 m/c hours per batch × 40 batches)	500
	935

$$\text{Cost driver rate} = \frac{£2,100}{935 \text{ m/c hours}} = £2.246 \text{ per m/c hour}$$

Machinery cleaning

	Set-ups
R (3 set-ups per batch × 36 batches)	108
S (2 set-ups per batch × 10 batches)	20
T (5 set-ups per batch × 40 batches)	200
	328

$$\text{Cost driver rate} = \frac{£800}{328 \text{ set-ups}} = £2.439 \text{ per set-up}$$

Calculation of the standard number of cost drivers for the actual output

	R	S	T	Total
Power	(1.4 × 30)	(1.7 × 12)	(0.8 × 40)	94.4 kJ
Stores	(5 × 30)	(3 × 12)	(7 × 40)	466 purchase orders
Maintenance	(10 × 30)	(7.5 × 12)	(12.5 × 40)	890 machine hours
Machinery cleaning	(3 × 30)	(2 × 12)	(5 × 40)	314 machine set-ups
Indirect labour (as per question)				

Flexed budget

Cost based on activity	£
Power (£12.5754 × 94.4)	1,187
Stores (£3.7755 × 466)	1,759
Maintenance (£2.246 × 890)	1,999
Machinery cleaning (£2.439 × 314)	766
Indirect labour (as per question)	1,387

(ii)

Production overhead budgetary control report – April 2001

	Original budget	Flexed budget	Actual	Variance
	£'000	£'000	£'000	£'000
Power	1,250	1,187	1,295	108 (A)
Stores	1,850	1,759	1,915	156 (A)
Maintenance	2,100	1,999	2,100	101 (A)
Machinery cleaning	800	766	870	104 (A)
Indirect labour	1,460	1,387	1,510	123 (A)
	7,460	7,098	7,690	592 (A)

8.7 (a) Overheads absorbed on machine hour basis

Machine hour absorption rate = Total overheads/Total machine hours

$$= \frac{£10,400 + £5,520 + £3,600 + £2,100 + £4,620}{(120 \times 4) + (100 \times 3) + (80 \times 2) + (120 \times 3)}$$

$$\frac{£26,000}{1,300} = £20 \text{ per machine hour}$$

Total costs based on machine hour basis

	A	B	C	D
	£	£	£	£
Direct materials	40	50	30	60
Direct labour	28	21	14	21
Production overhead	80	60	40	60
Production cost/unit	148	131	84	141
Output in units	120	100	80	120
Total production cost	£17,760	£13,100	£6,720	£16,920

(b) Overheads absorbed based on ABC

			Overhead costs	
	£	Level of activity	Cost/activity
Machine department cost	10,430	1,300	£8.02/hour
Set-up costs	5,250	21*	£250.00/run
Stores receiving costs	3,600	80**	£45.00/requisition
Inspection/quality costs	2,100	21*	£100.00/run
Material handling and despatch	4,620	42	£110.00/order

Workings

*No of production runs = output in units/20

$$= \frac{120 + 100 + 80 + 120}{20}$$

$$= \frac{420}{20} = 21$$

**No of requisition raised = No. of products × 20

$$= 4 \times 20 = 80$$

Total costs based on ABC

	A	B	C	D
	£	£	£	£
Direct materials	40.00	50.00	30.00	60.00
Direct labour	28.00	21.00	14.00	21.00
Machine dept costs	32.09	24.07	16.05	24.07
Set-up costs	12.50	12.50	12.50	12.50
Stores receving	7.50	9.00	11.25	7.50
Inspection	5.00	5.00	5.00	5.00
Material handling	11.00	11.00	11.00	11.00
Production cost/unit	136.09	132.57	99.80	141.07
Output in units	120	100	80	120
Total production costs	£16,331	£13,257	£7,984	£16,928

(c) Comparison of the two unit costs calculated in (a) and (b) above.

Product	A	B	C	D
	£	£	£	£
Based on machine hour rate	148.00	131.00	84.00	141.00
ABC method	136.09	132.57	99.80	141.07
Difference	111.91	(1.57)	(15.80)	(0.07)

Products A and C have the largest differences. The ABC approach in theory, attributes the cost of resources to each product which uses those resources on a more appropriate basis than the traditional method. The implication is that product A is more profitable than the traditional approach implies, whereas C is less profitable. If selling prices were determined on costs based on the traditional absorption method, the organisation might consider increasing the price of C and reducing that of A.

Learning Curves

Learning Curves

9

The learning effect reflects that as employees repeat a task they get faster at it.

The learning effect has implications for:

- Budgeting – the labour hours required for a given production level will fall over time.
- Capacity – if the total labour hours are fixed then output will increase over time.
- Costing – unit costs will fall with time.
- Pricing – prices below cost at the start of the life cycle may be above cost once learning has an effect.
- Decision-making – the annual cost of production will fall if output levels are fixed.

π   To calculate labour time, use the following relationship:

As total production doubles, cumulative average time per unit falls to a fixed percentage of its previous value.

This fixed percentage is called a learning rate.

It is expressed as the following formula:

$$y = ax^b$$

where,
y = cumulative average time per unit
x = cumulative production
a = time for first unit
b = index of learning $= \dfrac{\log(\text{learning rate})}{\log 2}$

When learning stops it is known as the steady state.

？ Questions

9.1   GH plc has received an order to make eight units of product K. The time to produce the first unit is estimated to be 100 hours and an 80% learning curve is expected. The rate of pay is £6 for each hour.

The direct materials for each unit is £2,500 and the fixed costs associated with the order are £9,600.

What is the average cost of each unit (to the nearest £) for this order of product K?

A £4,007
B £4,180
C £6,158
D £10,160
E £12,407

(3 marks)

9.2 BT plc has recently developed a new product. The nature of BT plc's work is repetitive and it is usual for there to be a 75% learning effect when a new product is developed. The time taken for the first unit was 2 hours. Four units have so far been made and sold to an existing customer. These four units included the first unit that took 2 hours to make.

A new customer has asked BT plc to supply an additional four units of the new product. If the labour rate is £12 per hour, how much should BT plc include in the price quotation in respect of labour cost?

(4 marks)

9.3 Data relating to the production of the first 32 batches of a new product are as follows:

Cumulative number of batches	Cumulative total hours
1	1,562.5
32	12,800

What is the percentage learning effect?

(3 marks)

9.4 Which of the following conditions must exist for there to be a learning curve effect?

(i) The task must be repetitive.
(ii) There must be a significant machine-based element to the work.
(iii) Production must be at an early stage or even be a new product.
(iv) The workforce is motivated to achieve improvements.
(v) There can be extensive breaks in production.

(2 marks)

9.5 The following diagram represents the learning curve effect:

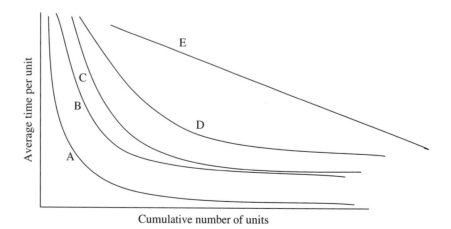

Cumulative number of units

Which of the curves illustrates the lowest learning effect?

(2 marks)

9.6   T plc has developed a new product, the TF8. The time taken to produce the first unit was 18 minutes. Assuming that an 80% learning curve applies, what time should be allowed for the fifth unit (to 2 decimal places)?

Note: For an 80% learning curve $y = ax^{-0.3219}$

(4 marks)

9.7   The following statements concern the learning effect.

When the steady state is reached,

  (i)   the total time stops rising.
  (ii) the cumulative average time stops falling.
  (iii) the marginal time stops falling.

Which of these statements is true?

(2 marks)

9.8   A company is preparing a quotation for a new product. The time taken for the first unit of the product was 30 minutes and the company expects an 85% learning curve. The quotation is to be based on the time taken for the final unit within the learning period which is expected to end after the company has produced 200 units.

Calculate the time per unit to be used for the quotation.

Note: The learning index for an 85% learning curve is -0.2345

(4 marks)

9.9   PR plc (IMPM 5/02 (Amended))

PR plc is a marketing consultancy company that offers three different types of service. It is preparing the budget for the year ending 31 December 2002. The details for each type of service are as follows:

	Service A	Service B	Service C
Estimated demand (number of services)	150	800	200
	£ per service	*£ per service*	*£ per service*
Fee income	2,500	2,000	3,200
Consultant (£300 per day)	900	750	1,500
Specialists' report	400	200	500
Variable overhead	200	160	300

It has been estimated that the consultants will be able to work for a total of 2,400 days during the year. PR plc estimates that the fixed overhead for the year will be £600,000.

Requirements

(a) (i) Prepare calculations that show how many of each type of service should be undertaken in order for PR plc to maximise its profits.

(ii) Prepare a statement that shows the budgeted profit for the year 2002 based on your answer to (i) above.

(8 marks)

The Managing Director has received the service schedule and budget statement that you prepared but would like it to be amended to reflect the following additional information:

– There is a 90% learning curve operating on the consultants' times for service C. The budgeted consultants' time of five days per service C was based on the time taken for the very first service C performed. By the end of December 2001, a total of 100 type C services will have been performed.
– The consultants' salaries will rise by 8% with effect from 1 January 2002.
– Overhead costs will rise by 5% with effect from 1 January 2002.

(b) Calculate the revised optimal service plan and prepare the associated profit statement for the year ending 31 December 2002.

(12 marks)

Note: The formula for a 90% learning curve is $y = ax^{-0.1520}$

(c) Explains the implications of the learning curve effect on service C for PR plc.

(5 marks)

(Total = 25 marks)

 Answers

9.1   If we can find the total cost of making all eight units we can then divide by eight to get the average cost per unit.

Direct materials cost will be = 8 units × £2,500 = £20,000

Fixed costs = £9,600

Labour cost:

Given that there is a learning effect, we must find the total time that is expected to manufacture all eight units.

We can use the law which says that as cumulative output doubles, the *average* time per unit is multiplied by the learning effect percentage.

Going from production of one unit to production of eight units, output doubles three times (1 becomes 2, 2 becomes 4, 4 becomes 8)

First unit produced: average time taken = 100 hours

So to produce eight units:

Average time per unit = 100 hours × 0.8 × 0.8 × 0.8 = 51.2 hours

Given that there are eight units,

Total time = 51.2 hours × 8 units = 409.6 hours

Therefore, labour cost = 409.6 hours × £6 = £2,457.60

So, direct materials cost will be = 8 units × £2,500 = £20,000

Fixed costs = £9,600

Labour cost = £2,457.60

Total cost = £20,000 + £9,600 + £2,457.60 = £32,057.60

Therefore, average cost per unit = £32,056.60/8 units = £4,007.20

9.2   We can work out the time taken to produce all 8 units that will then have been made using the law which says that as cumulative output doubles, the *average* time per unit is multiplied by the learning effect percentage. We will then need to deduct the time taken to produce the first 4 units in order to arrive at the time expected to be needed for the units to be made for the new customer.

We *cannot* just look at the latter 4 units. We *must* find the time for all 8 units and then deduct the time for the first 4 units.

Time for first 4 units already made and sold:

Going from production of 1 unit to production of 4 units, output doubles *twice* (1 becomes 2, 2 becomes 4)

So,
Average time per unit = 2 hours $\times$ 0.75 $\times$ 0.75 = 1.125 hours

Therefore, time taken for all 4 units = 4 units $\times$ 1.125 hours = 4.5 hours

Now for the time for first 8 units:

Going from production of 1 unit to production of 8 units, output doubles *three* times (1 becomes 2, 2 becomes 4, 4 becomes 8)

So,
Average time per unit = 2 hours $\times$ 0.75 $\times$ 0.75 $\times$ 0.75 = 0.84375 hour

Therefore, time taken for all 8 units = 8 units $\times$ 0.84375 hour = 6.75 hours

So, time for *latter* 4 units for new customer = 6.75 hours less 4.5 hours = 2.25 hours

Labour cost = 2.25 hours $\times$ £12 = £27

9.3   To calculate the learning effect percentage we need to use the law which says that as cumulative output doubles, the *average* time per unit is multiplied by the learning effect percentage.

Going from production of 1 unit to production of 32 units, output doubles five times (1 becomes 2, 2 becomes 4, 4 becomes 8, 8 becomes 16, then 16 becomes 32)

First unit produced: average time taken = 1,562.5 hours

32 units produced: average time taken = 12,800 hours/32 units = 400 hours

Let's suppose the learning effect rate is $L\%$

So,
$1{,}562.5 \times L \times L \times L \times L \times L = 400$

That is,
$1{,}562.5 \times L^5 = 400$

$L^5 = 400 \div 1{,}562.5 = 0.256$

So,

$L = \sqrt[5]{0.256}$

$L = 0.761$

That is, the learning effect rate is 76.1%

Say, 76%

9.4   (i)   Is correct. The task involved must be repetitive so that workers can learn to become quicker.

    (ii)   Is incorrect. There must be a significant manual or labour-based element to the work, NOT a significant machine-based element.

    (iii)   Is correct. If the product had been made for a long period of time, any learning effect would already have happened and time taken to make each unit would have settled down to a "steady state".

    (iv)   Is correct. Motivated workers will strive to become better at producing a new or fairly new product, whereas de-motivated workers will not.

    (v)   Is incorrect. If there are extensive breaks in production, workers will "forget" the skills learned and have to go through a learning effect again once work recommences.

9.5   The shallowest curve which bottoms out last (i.e. reaches a "steady state" last) exhibits the lowest learning curve percentage.

This is, therefore, Curve E.

9.6   Unfortunately, we cannot use the learning curve law which says that as cumulative output doubles, the *average* time per unit is multiplied by the learning effect percentage, since to find the time taken for 5 units does not fall into a pattern of doubling up production levels. (Having produced one unit, doubling production levels would double from 1 to 2 units, then 2 to 4 units, then 4 to 8 units.)

Therefore we must use the learning curve equation. This is the reason why the equation has been given to us in the question.

In fact, to find the time taken for the 5th unit, we must find the time to produce all 5 units and then deduct the time taken to produce the first 4 units. We cannot just look at the fifth unit in isolation.

Time for all 5 units:

Using the equation with number of units x being 5

$y = ax^{-0.3219}$

where, "y" is the *average* time per unit produced and "a" is the time taken for the first unit.

So,

$y = ax^{-0.3219} = 18$ multiplied by $5^{-0.3219} = 18$ multiplied by 0.5956

$y = 10.72$ min

So, time taken for all 5 units = 10.72 min $\times$ 5 units = 53.60 min

Time for first 4 units:

Using the equation with number of units x being 4

$y = ax^{-0.3219}$

where "y" is the *average* time per unit produced and "a" is the time taken for the first unit.

So,

$y = ax^{-0.3219}$
$= 18$ multiplied by $4^{-0.3219}$
$= 18$ multiplied by 0.64

$y = 11.52$ min

So, time taken for first 4 units = 11.52 min $\times$ 4 units = 46.08 min

Therefore, time taken for the 5th unit is:

53.6 min $-$ 46.08 min = 7.53 min

9.7   When the steady state is reached each unit takes the same amount of time as the last one, thus the marginal time is constant. The total time will continue to rise and the average time will continue to fall (albeit at a reduced rate).

9.8 $y = ax^b$

At 200 units: $y = 30 \times 200^{-0.2345} = 8.660$
Total time = $8.660 \times 200 =$ 1,732.00 minutes

At 199 units: $y = 30 \times 199^{-0.2345} = 8.670$
Total time = $8.670 \times 199 =$ 1,725.33 minutes

The time for the 200th unit to be used for the quotation is **6.67 minutes**

9.9

(a) (i)

Service type	A	B	C
Contribution/service	£1,000	£890	£900
Consultant days/service	3	2.5	5
Contribution/consultant day	£333.30	£356.00	£180.00
Ranking	2nd	1st	3rd
Demand/usage in services	133*	800	0
Days used	400	2,000	0

* Restricted due to lack of consultant days.

(ii)

Service type	A	B	C	Total
Number of each service	133	800	NIL	
	£	£	£	£
Fee charged/service	2,500	2,000	3,200	
Variable cost/service	(1,500)	(1,110)	(2,300)	
Contribution/service	1,000	890	900	
Total contribution	133,000	712,000	NIL	845,000
Fixed costs				(600,000)
Profit				245,000

(b) *Learning curve*:

Project C time per service = 5 days. The time taken for the first service is 5 days so the average time for 100 services and 300 services are:

For 100 Services $y = ax^{-b}$

where,
a is the time for the first service
x is the cumulative number of services
b equals 0.1520
$y = 5 \times 100^{-0.1520} = 2.483$ days

For 300 Services $y = 5 \times 300^{-0.1520} = 2.101$ days

Thus the total time taken:

300 services $\times$ 2.101 = 630.30
100 services $\times$ 2.483 = 248.30
Total time for 200 services in 2002 = 382 days

The learning curve effect changes the ranking of the services:

Service type	A £	B £	C £
Fee charged	2,500	2,000	3,200
Consultant	972	810	619*
Specialist's report	400	200	500
Variable overhead	210	168	315
	1,582	1,178	1,434
Contribution	£918	£822	£1,766
Consultant days/service	3	2.5	1.91*
Contribution/consultant day	£306.00	£328.80	£924.60
Ranking	3rd	2nd	1st
Demand/usage in services	6**	800	200
Days used	18	2,000	382

* Based on average consultant days for the 200 services.

** Restricted due to lack of consultant days.

Service type	A	B	C	Total
Number of services	6	800	200	n/a
	£	£	£	£
Fee charged	15,000	1,600,000	640,000	2,255,000
Consultant's time	5,832	648,000	123,768	
Specialist's report	2,400	160,000	100,000	
Variable overhead	1,260	134,400	63,000	
	9,492	942,400	286,768	1,238,660
Contribution	5,508	657,600	353,232	1,016,340
Fixed costs				630,000
Profit				386,340

(c) There are a number of implications of the learning curve, both in general, and with specific relevance to service C.

When comparing the actual performance results from service C against the planned performance, it is realistic to make allowance in the plan for the anticipated effects of the 90% learning curve.

There may also be a learning effect on the usage of the other resources associated with service C. These effects have not been allowed for in the standard costs and thus, unless they are recognised as learning effects, these will give rise to variances that will be reported as operating variances.

The learning curve implications must also be considered from the point of view of the scheduling and planning resource utilisation. As can be seen from the earlier calculations, the effect of the learning curve can significantly affect the optimal utilisation of scarce resources.

Finally, if selling prices are based on costs that do not consider the effects of the learning curve, services can be overpriced, resulting in low demand, which will increase average time per service due to the lower cumulative number of services.

Costing Systems

Costing Systems

10

Throughput accounting (TA)

Based on the 'theory of constraints', throughput accounting is a method of assessing performance which is most appropriate when a company faces production constraints (often referred to as bottlenecks).

It is used to try to maximise the rate at which a company can generate profits. It does this by focussing on maximising throughput, minimising stock and controlling costs.

Throughput contribution = sales revenue − material costs

Note that only material costs are considered variable in the short term.

Key measures

$$\text{Return per hour on bottlenect} = \frac{\text{throughput contribution}}{\text{hours on bottleneck}}$$

TA ratio = Throughput contribution in period/Conversion costs in period where conversion costs are labour and overhead.

Note: The TA ratio is often calculated as:

$$\frac{\text{throughput per hour}}{\text{conversion costs per hour}},$$

which gives the same result.

This ratio must be greater than one (>1) for the organisation to be profitable.

Backflush accounting

A simplified double entry system for production costs which is suitable for JIT and TQM systems.

Based on 'trigger points', actions that trigger a double entry.

A three trigger point system would record the purchase of materials, *not* the movement or processing of materials, just their completion and sale.

Purchases

Dr Raw materials and in process account
Cr Creditors/cash

Issue to production/movements between processes

No entries.

Items completed

Dr Finished goods account
Cr Raw materials and in-process account
 – with standard material cost of completed items.

Dr Finished goods account
Cr Labour
 – with standard labour cost of completed items.

Similarly with overheads.

Items sold

Normal entries

The big advantage is the simplicity of the system and its associated cost saving.

The disadvantages are the loss of information regarding inventory and losses – this is considered a small cost in JIT and TQM environments.

Target costing

This is a reversal of the traditional cost plus pricing system where the selling price is based on existing cost levels plus a mark-up. In target costing the starting point is the selling price, appropriate profits are then deducted and the result is the target cost.

The company should improve its customer focus (by starting with the customer) as well as improving cost control (costs increases cannot be passed on to the customer). In essence the product is designed around the cost.

Life cycle costing

Increasingly companies are finding that costs of new products are incurred in the early stages of the life cycle. Traditional reporting systems tend to use arbitrary time periods to match costs and revenues. Life cycle costing attempts to match costs with revenues over whatever time period is appropriate.

Making this link enables a company to properly ascertain the overall profitability of a product and improve future decision-making.

? Questions

10.1 Which of the following statements is not true of throughput accounting?

   A   Throughput accounting considers that the only variable costs in the short run are materials and components.

   B   Throughput accounting considers that time at a bottleneck resource has value, not elsewhere.

   C   Throughput accounting views stock building as a non-value-adding activity, and therefore discourages it.

   D   Throughput accounting was designed as a decision-making tool for situations where there is a bottleneck in the production process.

(2 marks)

10.2 Which of the following is a definition of the throughput accounting ratio?

   A   Throughput contribution ÷ hours on bottleneck
   B   Conversion costs per hour ÷ throughput per hour
   C   Throughput per hour ÷ conversion costs per hour
   D   Total conversion costs ÷ total throughput

(2 marks)

10.3 The following statements all concern Backflush accounting.

   (i)   Backflush accounting is good at identifying abnormal losses in a system.
   (ii)   Backflush accounting is primarily a recording system used as part of double entry.
   (iii)   Backflush accounting is well suited for use in JIT systems.

Which of these statements are substantially true?

(2 marks)

10.4 Calculate the throughput accounting ratio for the following product.

Units produced		500
Time taken		200 hours
Maximum time available		200 hours
Materials purchased	1,000 kg costing	£3,000
Materials used		800 kg
Labour costs		£2,000
Overheads		£1,500
Sales		£9,000

(2 marks)

10.5 A company has recently adopted throughput accounting as a performance measuring tool. Its results for the last month are shown below.

Units produced		1,150
Units sold		800
Materials purchased	900 kg costing	£13,000
Opening material inventory used	450 kg costing	£7,250
Labour costs		£6,900
Overheads		£4,650
Sales price		£35

There were no opening inventory of finished goods or closing inventory of materials.

What is the throughput accounting ratio for this product?

(3 marks)

10.6 What is backflush accounting and what are its limitations?

(5 marks)

10.7 What are the aims of throughput accounting and what are its limitations?

(5 marks)

10.8 A laboratory which does blood testing is intending to use ABC system to obtain accurate information regarding the three tests undertaken.

It has maintenance costs of £105,650 which are related to the equipment used for the testing of the blood. The cost driver for the maintenance expenditure is taken as the number of stages in tests undertaken.

Information about each test and the number of stages required is given below.

Test	GL	BD	XS
Total tests undertaken	7,000	2,000	4,000
Number of stages	4	3	1

What is the maintenance cost for each test of type BD?

(2 marks)

10.9 Grant plc has struggled with low profits in recent years and so is undertaking a major overhaul of its systems. It is replacing its production process with a more highly automated one and adopting a target costing approach.

A summary of the changes is given below.

	Current system	New system
Selling price	£41	£35
Variable cost per unit	£26	£8
Fixed cost per annum (excluding depreciation)	£185,000	?
Capital equipment	£1.7m	£4.4m
Life expectancy	5 years	8 years
Sales volume	40,000 per annum	90,000 per annum

The company holds no inventory and uses straight line depreciation.

What is the target fixed cost (excluding depreciation) for annual production if the company intends to achieve five times its current profit?

(3 marks)

10.10 A company is changing its costing system from traditional absorption costing (AC) based on labour hours to ABC system.

It has overheads of £156,000 which are related to taking material deliveries.

The delivery information about each product is given below.

Product	X	Y	Z
Total units required	1,000	2,000	3,000
Delivery size	200	400	1,000

Total labour costs are £360,000 for 45,000 hours. Each unit of each product takes the same number of direct hours.

Assuming that the company uses the number of deliveries as its cost driver, calculate the increase or decrease in unit costs for Z arising from the change from AC to ABC.

(3 marks)

10.11 The following statements relate to the justification of the use of life cycle costing.

(i) Product life cycles are becoming increasingly short. This means that the initial costs are an increasingly important component in the product's overall costs.

(ii) Product costs are increasingly weighted to the start of a product's life cycle, and to properly understand the profitability of a product these costs must be matched to the ultimate revenues.

(iii) The high costs of (for example) research, design and marketing in the early stages in a product's life cycle necessitate a high initial selling price.

(iv) Traditional capital budgeting techniques do not attempt to minimise the costs or maximise the revenues over the product life cycle.

Which of these statements are substantially true?

(2 marks)

10.12 A company is designing a new version of its best selling product, to be called "Widget4u". Estimated information regarding this product is shown below.

Design costs (viewed as capital)	£62,000
Production equipment costs	£784,000
Annual fixed costs (excluding depreciation)	£28,000
Variable costs	£8 per unit
Selling price	£34 per unit
Target sales	15,000 units per annum
Life	5 years
Required return on capital	12%

What is the target cost for annual production?

(3 marks)

10.13 LM Hospital (IDEC 5/01 (Amended))

LM Hospital is a private hospital, whose management is considering the adoption of an ABC system for the year 2001/02. The main reason for its introduction would be to provide more accurate information for pricing purposes. With the adoption of new medical technology, the amount of time that some patients stay in hospital has decreased considerably, and the management feels that the current pricing strategy may no longer reflect the different costs incurred.

Prices are currently calculated by determining the direct costs for the particular type of operation and adding a mark-up of 135%. With the proposed ABC system, the management expects to use a mark-up for pricing purposes of 15% on cost. This percentage will be based on all costs except facility sustaining costs. It has been decided that the hospital support activities should be grouped into three categories – admissions and record keeping, caring for patients and facility sustaining.

The hospital has four operating theatres that are used for 9 hours a day for 300 days a year. It is expected that 7,200 operations will be performed during the coming year. The hospital has 15 consultant surgeons engaged in operating theatre work and consultancy. It is estimated that each consultant surgeon will work at the hospital for 2,000 hours in 2001/02.

The expected costs for 2001/02 are:

	£
Nursing services and administration	9,936,000
Linen and laundry	920,000
Kitchen and food costs (3 meals a day)	2,256,000
Consultant surgeons' fees	5,250,000
Insurance of buildings and general equipment	60,000
Depreciation of buildings and general equipment	520,000
Operating theatre	4,050,000
Pre-operation costs	1,260,000
Medical supplies – used in the hospital wards	1,100,000
Pathology laboratory (where blood tests etc. are carried out)	920,000
Updating patient records	590,000
Patient / bed scheduling	100,000
Invoicing and collections	160,000
Housekeeping activities, including ward maintenance, window cleaning, etc.	760,000

Other information for 2001/02:

Nursing hours	480,000
Number of pathology laboratory tests	8,000
Patient days	44,000
Number of patients	9,600

Information relating to specific operations for 2001/02:

	ENT (Ear, nose and throat)	Cataract
Time of stay in hospital	4 days	1 day
Operation time	2 hours	0.5 hour
Consultant surgeon's time (which includes time in the operating theatre)	3 hours	0.85 hour

Requirement

Before making the final decision on the costing/pricing system, management has selected two types of operation for review: an ENT operation and a cataract operation.

Calculate the prices that would be charged under each method for the two types of operation. (Your answer should include an explanation and calculations of the cost drivers you have used.)

(10 marks)

10.14 Openroad plc is a manufacturer of caravans and campervans. It has been in business for many years, and has recently invested heavily in automated processes. It continues to use a total costing system for pricing, based on recovering overheads by a labour hour absorption rate.

Openroad plc is currently experiencing difficulties in maintaining its market share. It is therefore considering various options to improve the quality of its caravans and campervans, and the quality of its service to its customers. It is also investigating its present pricing policy, which is based on the costs attributed to each van.

Requirement

Explain the benefits (or otherwise) that an ABC system would give Openroad plc.

(10 marks)

10.15 KL (DM 11/06)

KL manufactures three products, W, X and Y. Each product uses the same materials and the same type of direct labour but in different quantities. The company currently uses a cost plus basis to determine the selling price of its products. This is based on full cost using an overhead absorption rate per direct labour hour. However, the Managing Director is concerned that the company may be losing sales because of its approach to setting prices. He thinks that a marginal costing approach may be more appropriate, particularly since the workforce is guaranteed a minimum weekly wage and has a three-month notice period.

The direct costs of the three products are shown below:

Product	W	X	Y
Budgeted annual production (units)	15,000	24,000	20,000
	$ per unit	$ per unit	$ per unit
Direct materials	35	45	30
Direct labour ($10 per hour)	40	30	50

In addition to the above direct costs, KL incurs annual indirect production costs of $1,044,000.

An analysis of the company's indirect production costs shows the following:

	$	Cost driver
Material ordering costs	220,000	Number of supplier orders
Machine setup costs	100,000	Number of batches
Machine running costs	400,000	Number of machine hours
General facility costs	324,000	Number of machine hours

The following additional data relate to each product:

Product	W	X	Y
Machine hours per unit	5	8	7
Batch size (units)	500	400	1,000
Supplier orders per batch	4	3	5

Requirements

(a) Given the Managing Director's concern about KL's approach to setting selling prices, discuss the advantages and disadvantages of marginal cost plus pricing AND total cost plus pricing.

(6 marks)

(b) Calculate the full cost per unit of each product using KL's current method of absorption costing.

(4 marks)

(c) Calculate the full cost per unit of each product using activity based costing.

(8 marks)

(d) Explain how activity-based costing could provide information that would be relevant to the management team when it is making decisions about how to improve KL's profitability.

(7 marks)
(Total = 25 marks)

10.16 MANPAC (IDEC 11/03)

SY Ltd, a manufacturer of computer games, has developed a new game called the MANPAC. This is an interactive 3D game and is the first of its kind to be introduced to the market. SY Ltd is due to launch the MANPAC in time for the peak selling season.

Traditionally SY Ltd has priced its games based on standard manufacturing cost plus selling and administration cost plus a profit margin. However, the management team of SY Ltd has recently attended a computer games conference where everyone was talking about life cycle costing, target costing and market-based pricing approaches. The team has returned from the conference and would like more details on the topics they heard about and how they could have been applied to the MANPAC.

Requirements

As Management Accountant of SY Ltd,

(a) Discuss how the following techniques could have been applied to the MANPAC:

- life cycle costing
- target costing.

(8 marks)

(b) Evaluate the market-based pricing strategies that should have been considered for the launch of the MANPAC and recommend a strategy that should have been chosen.

(6 marks)

(c) Explain each stage in the life cycle of the MANPAC and the issues that the management team will need to consider at each stage. Your answer should include a diagram to illustrate the product life cycle of the MANPAC.

(11 marks)
(Total = 25 marks)

10.17 Standard (IDEC 5/02)

Standard costing and target costing have little in common for the following reasons:

- the former is a costing system and the latter is not
- target costing is proactive and standard costing is not
- target costs are agreed by all and are rigorously adhered to, whereas standard costs are usually set without wide consultation.

Requirements

(a) Discuss the comparability of standard costing and target costing by considering the validity of the statements above.

(18 marks)

A pharmaceutical company, which operates a standard costing system, is considering introducing target costing.

(b) Discuss whether the company should do this and whether the two systems would be compatible.

(7 marks)
(Total = 25 marks)

✅ Answers

10.1 **D**

All of these points are true, except D.

Throughput accounting was designed as a performance measurement tool, not a decision-making tool.

One of its advantages is that it will be used by managers to make decisions that have outcomes that are goal congruent with corporate aims. However, it was designed as a performance measurement tool.

10.2 **C**

Answer C is the same as total throughput ÷ total conversion costs, which is an alternative, correct, definition (which gives the same value).

Answers B and D are the same: they are the correct ratio inverted.

Answer A is often referred to as the return per hour.

10.3 (i) Backflush accounting makes assumptions about the relationships between inputs and outputs, that is, for a given output it will assume the inputs are standard, therefore it cannot cope with unexpected losses.

(ii) It is a double entry system with reduced inventory entries.
(iii) Since there are few inventory records, BA copes well with JIT.

10.4 The throughput accounting ratio is defined as throughput ÷ total factory costs (these can both be calculated per hour, but that is, more work for the same answer!).

Throughput = sales − all material costs = £9,000 − £3,000 = £6,000
(Note that we use materials purchased instead of materials used.)

Total factory costs = all other production costs = £2,000 + £1,500 = £3,500

TA ratio = £6,000 ÷ £3,500 = 1.7.

10.5 The throughput accounting ratio is defined as throughput ÷ total factory costs.

Throughput accounting aims to discourage inventory building, so the ratios do not take account of inventory movements.

Throughput = sales − all material costs = £35 × 800 − £13,000 = £15,000
(Note that we use materials purchased instead of materials used.)

Total factory costs = all other production costs = £6,900 + £4,650 = £11,550

TA ratio = £15,000 ÷ £11,550 = 1.3.

10.6 Backflush accounting is a recording process used in manufacturing businesses (and similar) to record stocks and work in progress in the company. It forms part of the company's double entry system.

The double entries are made when inventory reaches "trigger points" in the process.

The main limitations of this are as follow:

Since entries are made at standard, it will fail to highlight any unexpected losses until a stock take is made. Backflush accounting is therefore most suitable in a TQM environment.

No record is kept of work in progress, leading to inventory being understated. This is not usually significant if the company operates a JIT system.

Records are not up to date – inventory is not recorded as leaving an area until it has reached the end of the process.

10.7 Throughput accounting was developed to help managers improve the overall profitability of the firm.

It focuses attention on constraints or bottlenecks within the organisation which hinder production. This main concept is to maximise the rate of manufacturing output, that is, the throughput of the organisation.

Throughput accounting is only appropriate where there are constraints on production, a company with spare capacity would find traditional techniques more appropriate.

Throughput accounting is not so well understandable as more traditional techniques.

Throughput accounting assumes that all factory costs are fixed, whilst this may be true for many of these costs, it is not true for, say, overtime costs.

10.8 *ABC*

Number of stages for GL	7,000 × 4	21,000
Number of stages for BD	2,000 × 3	6,000
Number of stages for XS	4,000 × 1	4,000
Total		31,000

| Cost per stage | £105,650 ÷ 31,000 | £3.41 |
| Cost per test of BD | £3.41 × 3 stages | £10.23 |

10.9 First we will calculate existing profit and multiply by 5. We can then look at the contribution required. Fixed costs need to include depreciation when calculating profit.

	£
Current contribution (41 − 26) × 40,000	£600,000
Current fixed costs £185,000 + £1.7m ÷ 5 years	£525,000
Current profit	£75,000
Expected contribution (35 − 8) × 90,000	£2,430,000
Target profit 5 × £75,000	£375,000
Target fixed costs	£2,055,000
Depreciation £4.4m ÷ 8 years	£550,000
Target fixed costs	£1,505,000

10.10 It is worth noting that the labour cost is not needed here: it is a direct cost and will not change, regardless of the method used.

We will calculate the overhead cost per unit under both systems and calculate the difference.

AC since the time per unit is the same for each product, the overheads per unit will also be the same.

£156,000 ÷ 6,000 units   £26
(you would get the same answer using labour hours)

ABC	Number of deliveries for X	1,000 ÷ 200	5
	Number of deliveries for Y	2,000 ÷ 400	5
	Number of deliveries for Z	3,000 ÷ 1,000	3
	Total		13

Cost per delivery	£156,000 ÷ 13	£12,000	
Cost per unit of Z	£12,000 ÷ 1,000 units		£4
Decrease	£26 − £12		£14

10.11 (i) This is true, justifying the time and effort of life cycle costing.

(ii) As above.

(iii) This is not true: life cycle costing is not about setting selling prices, it is about linking total revenues to total costs. Even if it were about setting a selling price, the early sales may well be at a loss since it is TOTAL revenues and costs that are considered. Furthermore, the pre-launch costs are sunk at launch and are therefore irrelevant when setting a selling price.

(iv) This is true. The deliberate attempt to maximise profitability is the key to life cycle costing.

10.12 The target cost is the expected sale proceeds less required profit. Note that the annual cost information (and depreciation) given is irrelevant.

		£
Expected revenue	£34 × 15,000	£510,000
Required profit	12% × (162,000 + 784,000)	£113,520
Target cost		£396,480

10.13 *Direct costs*:

Number of theatre hours	300 days × 4 theatres × 9 hours	10,800
Theatre cost per hour	£4,050,000 ÷ 10,800	£375
Pre-operation cost per operation	£1,260,000 ÷ 7,200	£175
Consultants' fees per hour	£5,250,000 ÷ (2,000 hours × 15)	£175

Indirect costs:

Caring for patients: £'000

Nursing	9,936
Linen and laundry	920
Kitchen and food	2,256
Medical supplies	1,100
Pathology laboratory	920
	15,132

Patient care cost per day = £15,132,000 ÷ 44,000 days = £343.91

Admissions and record keeping: £'000

Updating records	590
Patient/bed scheduling	100
Invoicing	160
	850

Admission costs per patient = £850,000 ÷ 9,600 patients = £88.54

Facility sustaining costs: £'000

Housekeeping	760
Insurance of buildings etc.	60
Depreciation of buildings etc.	520
	1,340

> ❗ The indirect costs have been split into the three categories indicated in the question. The chosen cost driver for caring for patients is patient days, on the grounds that most of the costs placed in this category are dependent on the length of patient stay. Medical supplies and pathology laboratory do not fit well into this category and a more accurate accounting treatment would have been given if the information had been available.
>
> The chosen cost driver for admissions and record keeping is number of patients, on the grounds that these costs vary with the number of patients rather than their length of stay or type of illness.
>
> Facility sustaining costs have not been given a cost driver because the question says that the mark-up is to cover these costs. Either treatment is acceptable under ABC.

Price for an ENT operation:

	Existing method	ABC	
	£	£	£
Direct costs:			
Operation £375 × 2 hours	750.00		
Pre-operation costs	175.00		
Consultant's fee £175 × 3 hours	525.00		
	1,450.00		1,450.00
Mark-up on direct costs 135%	1,957.50		
ABC (Support costs):			
Patient care cost £343.91 × 4 days		1,375.64	
Admission costs		88.54	
			1,464.18
			2,914.18
Mark-up 15%			437.13
Price	3,407.50		3,351.31

Price for a cataract operation:

	Existing method	ABC	
	£	£	£
Direct costs:			
Operation £375 × 0.5 hour	187.50		
Pre-operation costs	175.00		
Consultant's fee £175 × 0.85 hour	148.75		
	511.25		511.25
Mark-up on direct costs 135%	690.19		
ABC (Support costs):			
Patient care cost £343.91 × 1 day		343.91	
Admission costs		88.54	
			432.45
			943.70
Mark-up 15%			141.56
Price	1,201.44		1,085.26

10.14 An ABC system is a form of absorption costing that dispenses with the arbitrary labour hours (or similar) as a basis for absorption and replaces it with a more realistic system based on the activities that cause the costs.

The benefits of this to Openroad plc are set out below.

The cost split between products should be more realistic, helping to inform Openroad plc's management as to which products are using more of the company's productive resources.

An understanding of the activities that cause costs should help the management of Openroad plc to exercise better control over those activities and hence the costs.

Selling prices based on cost will now more realistically reflect the resources that went into producing the caravan or campervan being sold, helping to ensure that Openroad plc becomes (more) profitable.

The adoption of ABC system can be part of a wider scheme encouraging everyone to focus on their customer, as required by TQM and similar approaches. It is clear that sales staff have customers but it should also be apparent that the Management Accountant has customers: managers. Managers need accurate reliable relevant information to help them fulfil their roles, ABC system should help provide this.

An ABC system will reflect the change in the nature of production: traditional manufacturing had a large direct labour component and thus using labour hours to absorb overheads was realistic, a change to ABC system will reinforce to management the changes in the company.

As production becomes more customer focused, and customers demand ever more personalised products the complexity and diversity inherent in the system will be captured by the costing information.

Unfortunately ABC system suffers from some drawbacks.

It implies more than it can deliver: ABC system is still somewhat arbitrary. Managers may feel that this is the "correct" cost and make incorrect decisions because of this.

Activity-based costing is more complex and time consuming than traditional approaches. It is not clear that its benefits are sufficiently high to ensure that it covers its own costs.

On balance an ABC system will probably benefit the company but it would become much more powerful if combined with JIT and TQM production systems.

10.15

Topic being tested

Marginal cost plus pricing, total cost plus pricing, traditional absorption costing and activity-based costing.

Approach

Calculate the unit cost of each product using direct labour hours to absorb the overheads.

Calculate the unit cost of each product using ABC:

Find the cost per order/batch/machine hour for each type of cost.
Find the total cost of producing W, X, and Y based on the number of batches/orders/machine hours and use this to find the cost per unit.

Compare the results.

Solution

(a) Absorption costing is a costing system that attributes all production costs to individual cost units. As a consequence, its use as part of a cost plus pricing system should ensure that the company is profitable providing the volume of sales provides a mark-up that is sufficient to cover the non-production costs that are incurred.

Marginal costing is a costing system that only attributes variable production costs to the cost unit. Thus the percentage mark-up that is added as part of a cost plus pricing system must be sufficient to cover the fixed production overhead costs as well as the non-production overhead costs before any profit results.

Both systems are used in an environment where market-based pricing is either difficult or inappropriate, often because of the uniqueness of the product or service being provided. Thus cost plus pricing enables senior managers to delegate the price setting decision to operational managers.

Both systems have their own problems. The use of absorption cost means that the price is dependent at least in part on the method used to absorb the costs into each cost unit. Furthermore, it suggests that this is the cost of the individual item whereas in fact it includes costs that would continue to be incurred if the item, were not produced. Thus a manager may reject a sale because the customer is only prepared to pay a price which is less than the absorption cost, but in fact that price would be better than no sale because it exceeds the variable cost and thus makes a contribution to the fixed costs that would be incurred anyway.

The use of marginal costing identifies the variable cost of the item produced and thus provides a clear indication of the minimum price that should be charged so as to avoid a negative contribution. However this approach may mean that managers are persuaded to sell items at too low a price, so that the contribution earned is insufficient to cover the fixed costs of the business. Also it is very difficult to increase the price for a subsequent sale of the same item to the same customer, so the company may find it difficult to break out of the low price arena once they have entered it.

(b)

			Hours
Direct labour hours:	W	15,000 × 4	60,000
	X	24,000 × 3	72,000
	Y	20,000 × 5	100,000
			232,000

Absorption rate $1,044,000/232,000 $4.50 per direct labour hour

Product	W	X	Y
	$/unit	*$/unit*	*$/unit*
Direct material	35	45.0	30.0
Direct labour	40	30.0	50.0
Overhead	18	13.5	22.5
Total	93	88.5	102.5

(c) Cost driver rates:

	W	X	Y
Number of batches	30	60	20
Number of supplier orders	120	180	100
Number of machine hours (000)	75	192	140

Material ordering cost $220,000/400 = $550 per supplier order
   Machine setup cost $100,000/110 = $909 per batch
Machine running cost $400,000/407,000 = $0.9828 per machine hour
   General facility cost $324,000/407,000 = $0.7961 per machine hour

Note: The values shown in the table below are calculated using these cost driver rates. This causes minor differences compared to the total overhead cost because of roundings.

Product	W		X		Y	
	Total	*/unit*	*Total*	*/unit*	*Total*	*/unit*
	$	$	$	$	$	$
Direct materials		35		45		30
Direct labour		40		30		50
Material ordering	66,000		99,000		55,000	
Machine setups	27,270		54,540		18,180	
Machine running	73,710		188,698		137,592	
General facility	59,708		152,851		111,454	
	226,688	15	495,089	21	322,226	16
Total cost		90		96		96

(d) The above calculations show that the unit cost of product W is similar under both the current absorption and activity-based costing methods. However, there are significant differences in the unit costs of product X and product Y. This may provide an opportunity to change the selling prices of these products to reflect their true cost. As a result, profitability may be improved.

Activity-based costing recognises the causes of costs and attributes the costs to products depending on their utilisation of the activities that cause costs to be incurred. As a consequence, it is argued that the attribution of costs is less arbitrary than traditional absorption costing and leads to more accurate unit costs.

The management of KL can use the information provided by the activity-based costing approach to identify potential cost savings by changing the method of operation within the company; for example by increasing the size of each batch or standardising on the material suppliers that are used to reduce the number of supplier orders. It may also be appropriate to consider investing in new machines to reduce the number of machine hours.

The effect of activity-based costing is often to identify costs as being more controllable because their cause has now been identified. While some facility costs will remain and are truly fixed as they are not driven by any particular future activity, many of the other costs will now become variable depending on the number of times an activity is performed and therefore more controllable.

10.16 *Tutorial note*: This answer is longer than would be expected of students in the time available, but illustrates the main issues that should be addressed.

(a) *Life cycle costing*

Life cycle costing involves identifying the costs and revenues over a product's life, that is, from inception to decline. Life cycle costing aims to maximise the profit generated from a product over its total life cycle. Studies show that 80 to 90% of a product's costs are incurred or committed during the planning and design stage and any increase in time during these stages means an increase in cost and a reduction in profit. The-life-cycle costing's view is that the revenue generated from a product must not only cover the production costs, but must also cover the costs incurred in the pre- and post-production stages of planning and concept design, preliminary design, detailed design and testing and the distribution and customer service costs. The product design and production process is determined at an early stage and provides the basis of the production costs. These costs effectively become "locked in" early in the product's life and it is at these early stages that cost management can be most effectively exercised.

This is unlike the current system that SY Ltd uses in that the standard manufacturing cost, once established, is uplifted by adding an amount to cover the selling and-administration costs as well as a profit margin. The costs incurred during the planning and design stages are therefore ignored when pricing the MANPAC and these will be a significant element of the cost. Also, this approach reports costs and-revenues on a periodic basis and actually ignores the total profitability of the MANPAC over its total life cycle. Therefore, the current approach used by SY Ltd does not provide a complete overview of the return generated over the MANPAC's life.

If SY Ltd were to implement life cycle costing, it would provide an overview of the MANPAC's performance. This would provide vital information when assessing potential cost reduction opportunities as well as revenue extension opportunities for the game.

Target costing
Target costing is effectively part of a strategic profit planning system in that it seeks to control costs and manage profit over a product's life cycle. Unlike standard costing, it is not a costing system. The main objective of target costing is to minimise costs over the life cycle of a product without compromising quality, reliability and other customer requirements. SY Ltd currently uses standard costing which is a system whereby a predetermined cost is established for the MANPAC. Once the MANPAC goes into production, any deviations from the standard cost are measured through variance analysis. SY Ltd also uses the standard cost information to determine the standard selling price. Unlike target costing, the standard costing method used by SY Ltd is taking an inward-looking approach for both pricing and cost control which focuses attention on the short term rather than the long term.

If SY Ltd were to implement target costing, the development and design stages for the MANPAC would be used to determine the target selling price. In order to identify the target cost for the MANPAC, SY Ltd must first undertake some market research to determine the target selling price for the MANPAC. From this, a desired margin would be deducted in order to arrive at a target cost. If the target cost is less than the predicted actual cost, the MANPAC will go through aredesign stage until such time as the MANPAC can be delivered within the target cost. Ultimately, SY Ltd must be able to manufacture and deliver the MANPAC at a cost that will enable the desired profit margin to be achieved, that is, the target profit. SY Ltd should then continue to revise the target cost over the life of the MANPAC and therefore make an ongoing effort to reduce costs and maintain profit. Continually revising the target cost over the MANPAC's life will make the management of SY Ltd more cost-conscious and focused on maintaining profit margins.

(b) *Market-based pricing strategies*

Price skimming
This method of pricing sets high initial prices in an attempt to exploit those sections of the market which are relatively insensitive to price changes.

Penetration pricing
This method sets very low prices in the initial stages of a product's life cycle to gain rapid acceptance of the product and therefore a significant market share. This method of pricing is followed if a company wishes to discourage-new entrants to the market. There may also be significant economies of scale to be gained if the low pricing leads to high volume and therefore cost reduction.

Target pricing
This method would mean that SY Ltd would first undertake some market research to determine the target selling price for the MANPAC. As discussed above, it would then use this target selling price to arrive at a target cost.

Recommendation
As the MANPAC is the first of its type to the market, SY Ltd could pursue one of two strategies – market skimming or penetration pricing.

As demand for computer games is generally highly inelastic, SY Ltd would be-advised to follow a market skimming strategy and set a high price to take advantage of the new game and the timing of its launch. By doing this, it will exploit customers who are prepared to pay high prices so as to ensure that they have the latest games on the market. It will also be easier for SY Ltd to reduce the price if the product does not reach the level of demand required. It may assist SY Ltd in generating high initial cash flows which would shorten the payback period on the initial investment in the MANPAC which is normally quite long due to high planning and design costs. Also, like many computer games, the MANPAC is likely to have a short life cycle and therefore by setting a high price, SY Ltd will recover the development costs and make a profit more quickly. A skimming policy will also allow SY Ltd to cover any unforeseen cost increases or falls in demand after the novelty appeal has declined.

Furthermore, SY Ltd needs to ensure that it has some significant barriers to-entry to deter competitors from entering the market, for example patent protection, otherwise competitors may enter the market with a lower-priced game.

(c)

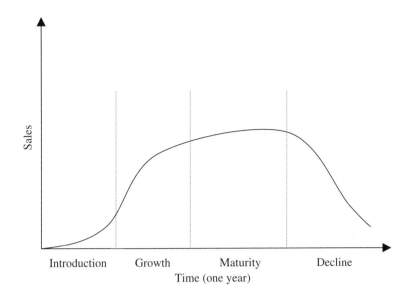

Product life cycle of the MANPAC

The product life cycle of the MANPAC is likely to be short. The life cycle of the MANPAC will significantly influence the pricing strategy. There are four stages in the life cycle:

1   Introduction
    The MANPAC is introduced to the market. Due to the nature of the MANPAC and the timing of its launch, it is likely that demand will be reasonably high (as indicated on the diagram). Also, assuming SY Ltd has already established a name in the market, it is likely that the MANPAC will gain market acceptance very quickly. The MANPAC will have already incurred significant costs in its planning, design, development and production stages and it is therefore vital that SY Ltd ensures that the MANPAC is marketed well so that its demand levels are high, otherwise they could stand to incur significant losses. The company therefore needs to ensure that it utilises its existing reputation when marketing the MANPAC.

2   Growth
    Assuming the MANPAC is accepted by the market and there has been a reasonable initial uptake (which would be expected at its peak selling season), the product will then enter the growth phase where demand for the MANPAC will increase. At this stage, the company will begin to experience lower costs due to the economies of scale resulting from the higher volume of sales. It is at this point that competitors might enter the market and SY Ltd may need to review its pricing strategy in order to remain competitive with comparable games in the market. It could either pursue a premium pricing strategy, an ongoing or average rate pricing strategy or a discount pricing strategy.

3   Maturity
    This is the stage where the MANPAC reaches the mass market and the increase in demand will begin to slow down. As can be seen in the diagram, the sales curve will begin to flatten out. If SY Ltd wishes to maintain demand for the MANPAC, it will need to consider some modification or improvements.

4 Decline

This is the point where the demand for the MANPAC begins to fall. At this point, SY Ltd will need to withdraw the MANPAC from the market and replace it with a new product. Stocks of the MANPAC could then perhaps be bundled with other games in an attempt to recover the costs of unsold units.

10.17

Examiner's note:

It is the quality of argument and points made that are important in this answer.

(a) Standard costing and target costing are similar techniques in so far as they are both concerned with the control of cost, but there are a number of differences between the two. The two major differences are:

the approach/attitude used – external/internal approach and the commitment of staff; and the timing of the control, which is illustrated below.

Proactive or not

Standard costing is normally used in a given situation, that is, when products have been in production for some time or when a new product is introduced and a detailed product design has already been produced and production methods determined. Standard times and quantities are determined for each unit and these are turned into costs. Control takes place once in every month when variances (between standard and actual) are calculated. The emphasis is placed on monitoring adverse variances and taking action to reduce these in the future. The selling price of a new product will be determined by estimating its standard cost and adding the required profit margin to the cost. Thus, standard costing is reactive rather than proactive.

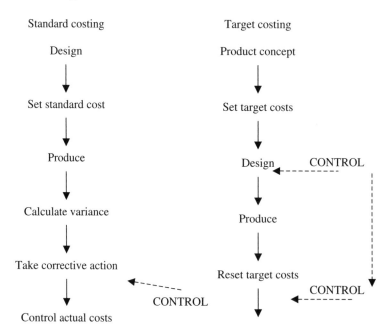

Target costing, on the other hand, is a proactive technique that starts before the design of the product is formalised. The starting point is market research on the price customers would be willing to pay for a product with various specified features. From this price, the required profit margin is deducted to leave a total target cost. This is then split down into a number of different costs for the different product functions. The product is then designed so that it can be manufactured within this cost. If this cannot be done, the product will not be produced. Once in production, the target cost is incorporated in the budgeting process and is reduced steadily over time. Hence, target costing is a cost reduction technique as well.

Agreed by all and rigorously adhered to
It may be untrue to suggest that more people are involved in setting target costs rather than standards, but generally people from a greater number of departments and areas of the business are involved, for example marketing and design. Neither system will work satisfactorily unless those who are responsible for cost have agreed to the target or standard cost. In Japan, where target costing originated, there is more of a consensus approach, which may have influenced the statement in the question. It can be argued that target costs are more rigorously adhered to as it is perceived by all that any increase in cost has a direct effect on profit. In addition, any Japanese manager exceeding the target, once the product is in production, is assigned a supervisory committee for six months to "help" him get the cost to the correct level.

Standard costs may not always be achieved if the situation has changed since the standard was set. For example, if the price of materials has increased, it may not be possible to reduce the actual material cost. This view may be accepted and the standard modified or a planning variance calculated. Furthermore, in some cultures, tight budgets are the norm and adverse variances expected.

Costing system
Whether both are costing systems depends on the definition of a costing system. The CIMA Terminology describes costing as "the process of determining the costs of products, services or activities". So, presumably, any method which determines costs could be called a costing system. This means that both standard costing and target costing could be considered costing systems.

Standard costing has always been considered a costing system because of its tie with budgeting, planning and control. As target costing is used in forecasting, and the Japanese use reducing target costs in their six-month budgets, there would appear to be no difference and both are, therefore, costing systems.

(b) The two systems were developed quite separately in different ages and in different parts of the world for different purposes. The aim of standard costing is to control future costs by looking at past costs and the aim of target costing is to control future costs by considering them in advance and limiting them to an acceptable level. Nevertheless, a company which uses standard costing could adapt the system to embrace the aims of a target costing system. The most important aspect would be to change the mindset of management to make them proactive rather than reactive. This could be quite difficult if target costing is seen simply as an "add-on".

A pharmaceutical company will have heavy research and development costs and a production which may start quite slowly in one market and expand to cover the world until the patent runs out. Because of the patent, there will have been little pressure on the company to control production costs until the patent runs out. (Research and development costs must, of course, be covered, but are usually covered many times on a successful product.) When the patent runs out, other companies can produce the product, but, by this time, doctors may be familiar with the name of the drug and may not switch to prescribing the cheaper drug. However, this scenario is changing and there is pressure on pharmaceutical companies to reduce prices in particular areas of the world where, for example, incomes are low. Therefore, target costing would have advantages because it would force the company to consider how to reduce future costs month by month, based on an experience curve and other factors.

If the pharmaceutical company's target costs are just "targets" rather than the "must achieve" level that the Japanese use, it would be dangerous to base standards on these and then reprimand managers if they did not achieve them. So the mindset behind the system is the important factor, rather than the name of the system, and a standard costing system with learning built in can be used to achieve precisely the same aims as a target costing system. Hence, they are compatible, but they would not be two separate systems. It would be possible to run two systems, but managers are likely to be confused by the difference between the standard cost and the target cost, with its main advantage of "must achieve", and so it is unlikely that many companies would decide to use both together.

The Principles of Budgeting

The Principles of Budgeting

11

Budgets have two main roles

1 They give authority to budget managers to incur expenditure in their part of the organisation.
2 They act as comparators for current performance, by providing a yardstick against which current activities can be monitored, and may be used as targets to motivate managers.

These two roles are combined in a system of budgetary planning and control.

Key requirements in the design of a budget plan

A good budgeting process would include

- A budgeting committee to co-ordinate the process
- The participation of all main budget holders
- The creation of a master budget to summarise all the functional budgets, comprising the budgeted income statement, budgeted balance sheet and budgeted cash flow statement.

Fixed budgets

A fixed budget is prepared under a given set of assumptions.

Steps

1 Identify the principal budget factor
2 Produce the budget for the principal budget factor
3 Produce the production budget
4 Other budgets.

Limiting factor analysis may be needed if the principal budget factor is anything other than sales.

Sensitivity analysis

A sensitivity analysis exercise involves revising the budget on the basis of a series of varied assumptions. In practical budgeting, there may be uncertainty concerning a large number of factors within the budget, and sensitivity analysis may consist of a series of complex 'what if?' enquires – reworking the budget, on the basis of a range of different scenarios.

Computer spreadsheets have made the task of carrying out sensitivity analysis much easier, but management must remain alert to the potential risks:

- Data integrity must be preserved, preferably by storing all data once only in a central data warehouse
- Standardised spreadsheets should be used to minimise errors
- Spreadsheets must be well designed such that the impact of any potential change will flow through the entire budget as soon as the assumption is altered.

Rolling budgets

Budgets are prepared on an ongoing basis, adding one month's budget to the end of a period as the current month passes.

These represent an attempt to replace the annual budgeting round with a system that spreads the workload more evenly and is inherently more up to date.

❓ Questions

11.1   In a manufacturing company each worker can produce four units per hour.

After units are produced they are inspected and 10% are typically found to be defective.
Workers spend four hours each per week on non-productive tasks.
The normal working week is 37 hours paid at £7.00/hour.
There are 25 workers.
Budget sales are 3,150 per week.

Any overtime is paid at time and a half.
The company holds no inventory.

What is the weekly labour cost budget?

(3 marks)

11.2   A company is expecting demand for its product to grow significantly, but is trying to constrain its growth in inventory.

Sales in January: 2,500 units
Inventory, 1st January: 500 units

Growth rate of sales: 25% per month.
Inventory policy: to grow at 15% per month.

What is the budgeted production in March?

(2 marks)

11.3 The following statements concern rolling budgets.

   (i) Rolling budgets are more able to deal with environmental uncertainty than traditional budgeting methods.

   (ii) Rolling budgets lead to a more evenly spread workload for the planners than traditional budgets.

   (iii) Rolling budgets produce more consistency as regards planning horizons than traditional budgeting techniques.

Which of these statements are substantially true?

(2 marks)

11.4 What is a rolling budget and when may it be more appropriate than traditional budgeting techniques?

(5 marks)

11.5 State why organisations prepare budgets.

(5 marks)

11.6 What is the principal budget factor and why is it essential to identify it at the start of the budgetary planning process.

(5 marks)

11.7 Give two potential disadvantages of participative budgeting.

(2 marks)

11.8 A manufacturing company has produced the budget for quarter 1 is as follows:

	£
Sales: 150 Units @ £30 per unit	4,500
Variable costs: 200 Units @ £15 per unit	(3,000)
Fixed costs	(1,000)
Profit	500

There is some uncertainty over the variable cost per unit. It is thought that it will be between £10 and £20, with £15 as the 'expected' outcome.

Carry out sensitivity analysis and comment on your results.

(8 marks)
(Total = 32 marks)

 **Answers**

11.1 Note that sales can only represent 90% of output, so we must multiply sales by 100/90 to get production.

Required good production = 3,150
Total production (3,150 × 100/90)	3,500 units

Total productive hours required (3,500 ÷ 4)	875 hours
Non-productive time (25 × 4)	100 hours
Total hours	975 hours

Normal hours available (25 × 37)	925 hours
Required overtime	50 hours

Normal cost (925 hours × £7)	£6,475
Overtime (50 hours × £7 × 150%)	£525
Total	£7,000

11.2 Since the growth rate of inventory is slower than sales we need to do a full budget.

	Jan	Feb	Mar
Sales	2,500	3,125	3,906
Opening inventory	(500)	(575)	(661)
Closing inventory	575	661	760
Production	2,575	3,211	4,005

11.3 A rolling budget with a three-month horizon would start a year with the budget for January, February and March already prepared. During January the April budget would be prepared, during February the May budget would be prepared, etc.

This means that

   (i)   budgets are prepared fairly close to when they are needed, leading to less need to predict an uncertain environment
   (ii) the workload is spread over the whole year
   (iii) the planning horizon is fixed (at three months in the example) rather than starting at 12+ months at the start of the year, and reducing as the year progresses.

11.4 A rolling budget is a budget prepared with a fixed planning horizon. To achieve this, the budget is constantly being added to at the same rate as time is passing.

For example, a company with a three-month rolling budget would start a new year with January–March's budget done. Then during January the April budget would be prepared, during February the May budget would be prepared, etc.

Rolling budgets can be very useful for companies experiencing rapid change, as they require forecasting for much shorter time periods.

Rolling budgets can also be useful for very seasonal businesses, especially where the peak of work is towards the year end as they spread the work out more evenly.

Rolling budgets are useful in dynamic environments where the nature of change is unpredictable. In these situations whole (12 month) budgets can be rendered obsolete by environmental change.

11.5 There are a number of reasons why organisations prepare budgets. These include

   • the formalisation of plans
   • the motivation of managers
   • the basis of comparison with actual performance
   • the need to coordinate activities
   • the anticipation of problems.

11.6 The principal budget factor is the factor that limits the activities of the organisation.

It must be identified at the start as it indicates which budget should be prepared first. Failure to do so could mean later delays when managers cannot meet targets set (for example where material purchases are insufficient to meet the production budget).

11.7 • It can result in a more extended and complex budgetary process.
   • There is a risk of budget slack where participants over-estimate costs and under-estimate revenues.

11.8 One approach to this would be to present the budget shown above as an 'expected' case but with two other cases as 'worst' and 'best' possible outcomes.

Worst-case budget (£20 Unit variable cost)

	£
Sales: 150 Units @ £30 per unit	4,500
Variable costs: 200 Units @ £20 per unit	(4,000)
Fixed costs	(1,000)
Profit/(loss)	(1,500)

Best-case budget (£10 Unit variable cost)

	£
Sales: 150 Units @ £30 per unit	4,500
Variable costs: 100 Units @ £10 per unit	(1,000)
Fixed costs	(1,000)
Profit	2,500

These results show that the worst-case scenario involves a loss of £1,500.

Management can now use this knowledge to improve their decision-making. They will probably wish to review the information used to predict variable costs to get a more accurate idea of the likely level.

They can then take action to ensure the worst-case scenario does not occur. They may decide to arrange for a fixed price contract for some of the materials, or switch supplier to save money. They may also instigate pay freezes or perhaps look to outsource production to save costs.

Budgetary Control

Budgetary Control

12

Systems approach

An organisation is a social system. Like other systems, it has inputs, a process and outputs.

Budgetary control is a form of feedback control in that it tries to identify (and thus correct) deviations from plan; it can be

- positive, to reinforce a beneficial deviation
- negative, to reduce a detrimental deviation.

Budgetary control is also a form of feedforward control in that it tries to anticipate deviations from planned performance.

Flexed budgets

A flexed budget is used to assess performance.

The original budget is adjusted (flexed) to take account of changes in activity levels and compared with actual costs.

- If costs are higher or revenues are lower than the budget, then the difference is an *adverse* variance.
- If costs are lower or revenues are higher than the budget, then the difference is a *favourable* variance.

Budget centre

A budget centre is a section of an entity for which control may be exercised through prepared budgets. It will have its own budget and a manager will be responsible for managing the centre and controlling the budget. The attribution of uncontrollable costs to budget centres should be minimised.

Managers should receive regular control information in the form of a budgetary control report.

175

Behavioural issues

Budgets are an attempt to direct staff. If they are not properly prepared they will demotivate staff.

In order to avoid this, the following should be true:

- Targets should be hard but achievable
- Rewards and incentives should be used to recognise good performance
- Staff should be allowed to participate in the budget-setting process
- Targets should be properly communicated to staff
- Staff alone should be held accountable for aspects of performance that they control
- Budgets should be goal congruent
- Budgets should cover more than just financial performance.

Budgets need to be flexed to actual activity level in order to properly assess performance; this is part of the control concept discussed above.

A budgetary control statement compares flexed budget with actual performance for each cost heading. This produces total variance figures.

Beyond Budgeting (BB)

Beyond Budgeting (BB) is the name given to a body of practices intended to replace budgeting as a management model. The core concept is the need to move from a business model based on centralised organisational hierarchies to one based on devolved networks.

BB is a 'responsibility model' whereby managers are given goals which are based on benchmarks linked variously to world class performance, peers, competitors and/or earlier periods. This requires an adaptive approach whereby authority is devolved to managers.

IT networks provide easy communication between different component parts of an organisation together with its customers, associates and suppliers. Quality programmes (TQM), process engineering (BPR), supply chain management (SCM), balanced scorecards and activity accounting all have a role.

Six main principles

1 Clear organisation structures
2 Goals and targets linked to relative success and shareholder value
3 Managerial freedom
4 Decisions that generate value taken by front line teams
5 Front line teams take responsibility for nurturing business relationships
6 Ethical and transparent information support systems.

❓ Questions

12.1 Company X makes widgets. The following information relates to the year just passed.

Standard cost of one widget =-£38
Actual cost of one widget = £39

Budget output = 5,150 widgets
Budget sales = 4,800 widgets
Actual output = 5,100 widgets
Actual inventory increase = 250 widgets.

There was no opening inventory.

What is the flexed budget cost of production?

(2 marks)

12.2 The widget company has been operating a standard costing system for some years. The following information relates to a recent year.

Budget output = 28,200 widgets
Budget inventory increase = 1,200 widgets

Actual inventory increase = 1,300 widgets
Actual sales = 28,900 widgets

Standard cost of one widget = £17
Actual cost of one widget = £15.

There was no opening inventory.

What is the flexed budget cost of production?

(2 marks)

12.3 What is feedback and feedforward control? Give an example of each from a budgeting perspective.

(5 marks)

12.4 Explain the concepts of positive and negative feedback. Give an example of each from a budgeting perspective.

(5 marks)

12.5 The purpose of a flexible budget is

    A   to cap discretionary expenditure.
    B   to produce a revised forecast by changing the original budget when actual costs are known.
    C   to control resource efficiency.
    D   to communicate target activity levels within an organisation by setting a budget in advance of the period to which it relates.

(2 marks)

12.6 In the context of budget preparation, the term "goal congruence" is

    A   the alignment of budgets with objectives using feedforward control.
    B   the setting of a budget which does not include budget bias.
    C   the alignment of corporate objectives with the personal objectives of a manager.
    D   the use of aspiration levels to set efficiency targets.

(2 marks)

12.7 Which of the following statements is/are true?

    (i)   A flexible budget can be used to control operational efficiency.
    (ii) Incremental budgeting is a system of budgetary planning and control that measures the additional costs of the extra units of activity.
    (iii) Participative budgeting is a method of centralised budgeting that uses a top-down approach and aspiration levels.

(2 marks)

12.8 What are the qualities of a good budgetary control report?

(5 marks)

12.9 What are the qualities of a good monthly management-accounting report?

(5 marks)

12.10 What are the main benefits of including managers in the budget-setting process?

(5 marks)

12.11 R plc is an engineering company that repairs machinery and manufactures replacement parts for machinery used in the building industry. There are a number of different departments in the company including a foundry, a grinding department, a milling department and a general machining department. R plc prepared its budget for the year ending 31 December 2003.

The budget is set centrally and is then communicated to each of the managers who has responsibility for achieving their respective targets. The following report has been produced for the general machining department for October 2003:

	Budget	Actual	Variance
Number of machine hours	9,000	11,320	2,320 (F)
	$	$	$
Cleaning materials	1,350	1,740	390 (A)
Steel	45,000	56,000	11,000 (A)
Other direct materials	450	700	250 (A)
Direct labour	29,000	32,400	3,400 (A)
Production overheads	30,000	42,600	12,600 (A)
Total	105,800	133,440	27,640 (A)

The Manager of the general machining department has received a memo from the Financial Controller, requiring him to explain the serious overspending within his department.

The Manager has sought your help and, after some discussion, you have ascertained the following:

- the cleaning materials, steel and other direct materials vary in proportion to the number of machine hours
- the budgeted direct labour costs include fixed salary costs of $4,250, the balance is variable in proportion to the number of machine hours
- the production overhead costs include a variable cost that is constant per machine hour at all activity levels, and a stepped fixed cost which changes when the activity level exceeds 10,000 machine hours. A further analysis of this cost is shown below:

Activity (machine hours)	3,000	7,000	14,000
Costs ($)	13,500	24,500	45,800

Requirements

Prepare a revised budgetary control statement using the additional information that you have obtained from the Manager of the general machining department. Comment on your findings.

(12 marks)

 # Answers

12.1 Do not forget that flexed budget is the *standard cost of actual output* = 5,100 × £38 = £193,800.

12.2 Do not forget that flexed budget is the *standard cost of actual output* = (28,900 + 1,300) × £17 = £513,400.

12.3 A feedback control involves obtaining information on actual results from the process and comparing with control data (a plan). Deviations from the control data will usually prompt control action in order to bring actual results back in line with plan.

Feedforward control works on the basis of forecast results; it is therefore anticipating problems and then dealing with them.

Traditional variance analysis is an example of a feedback control: actual costs are compared with a (flexed) budget and control action is taken.

Feedforward control usually takes place at the planning stage: if the cash budget forecasts that the overdraft limit is likely to be breached then remedial action is taken.

12.4 A feedback control involves obtaining information on actual results from the process and comparing with control data (a plan).

When the deviation from plan is considered undesirable then the control action is designed to reduce it. This is termed negative feedback.

When the deviation from plan is considered desirable then the control action is designed to increase it. This is termed positive feedback.

Generally an adverse variance will produce negative feedback: an adverse material price variance may reinforce the policy of bulk buying to obtain discounts.

Some favourable variances lead to positive feedback. For example, a customer care course might lead to sales exceeding budget in a branch: management would certainly consider extending this to other parts of the business.

12.5   **C**

    A   flexible budgets have no upper limit and therefore they do not act as a cap

    B   the original budget is adjusted for actual activity, not costs

    C   resource efficiency is controlled as the amount of resource used is only allowed to increase with activity levels

    D   activity levels will be flexed and therefore do not act as a target.

12.6   **C**

This is the definition of the term "goal congruence": the alignment of goals.

12.7   (i)   Flexible budgets ensure that resource usage does not rise disproportionately with activity, that is it does control efficiency.

    (ii)   Incremental budgeting does not look at extra units; it allows for an increment on previous budgets.

    (iii)   Participative budgeting is bottom up: it encourages input from more junior staff.

12.8   The qualities of a good budgetary control report are below.

Timely. The information should be made available as soon as possible after the end of the control period. Corrective action will be much more effective if it is taken soon after the event.

Accurate. Inaccurate control information could lead to inappropriate management action. There is often a conflict between the need for timeliness and the need for accuracy. The design of budgetary reporting systems should allow for sufficient accuracy for the purpose to be fulfilled.

Relevant. Busy managers should not be swamped with information that is not relevant to them. They should not need to search through a lot of irrelevant information to reach the part that relates to their area of responsibility.

Targeted. Control information should be directed to the manager who has the responsibility and authority to act upon it. If the information is communicated to the wrong manager its value will be immediately lost.

Understandable. Reports need to be understood by the person they are targeted at, this means avoidance of jargon and irrelevant information. Exception reporting may be used to keep the report clear from clutter.

12.9   A good monthly management-accounting report will have the following properties.

It will cover a range of predetermined financial performance measures, including budgets, standards and other financial requirements.

It will include aspects of non-financial performance such as service improvement targets and absenteeism.

It will direct attention to significant variations and to events that could produce significant deviations in the future.

It will represent the combination of very short-term reports available and of informal information systems, and should ensure that the manager directly involved can anticipate results.

It will act as an agenda, a way of structuring regular discussion of results, progress and plans, providing an overall view of all the activities.

12.10 The main benefits of involving managers in the budget-setting process include

- *Goal congruence.* The manager sees their organisational target as a personal target because, by their setting it, they believe it to be achievable.
- *Motivation.* The manager will be motivated to achieve the target, because not to do so would be a personal failure.
- *Accuracy/detail.* The manager will have the detailed knowledge to prepare a budget that accurately identifies the resource requirements needed to achieve the target set.

12.11 Clearly those costs that have a variable element need to be flexed before they are compared to actual. Each cost will be dealt with in turn and then a budgetary control statement will be produced.

Cleaning materials, steel and other direct materials are variable and can be flexed by multiplying by $11,320 \div 9,000$.

Analyse budget cost of direct labour:

	$
9,000 hours total cost	29,000
Fixed cost	(4,250)
Therefore variable cost of 9,000 hours	24,750

$$\text{Variable cost per hour} = \frac{\$24.750}{9,000} \$2.75$$

Therefore,

Budget cost of 11,320 hours:	$
Variable (11,320 × $2.75)	31,130
Fixed	4,250
	35,380

Use high/low technique to analyse production overheads (ignore 14,000 hours activity level to eliminate the effect of the step fixed cost):

	Hours	$
High	7,000	24,500
Low	(3,000)	(13,500)
Difference	4,000	11,000

$$\text{Variable cost per hour} = \frac{\$11.000}{4,000 \text{ hours}} = 2.75/\text{hour}$$

		$
Variable cost of 14,000 hours (14,000 × $2.75)	=	38,500
Total cost of 14,000 hours	=	45,800
Fixed cost (for activity levels above 10,000 hours)	=	7,300

	Original budget	Flexed budget	Actual	Variance
Number of machine hours	9,000	11,320	11,320	
	$	$	$	$
Cleaning materials	1,350	1,698	1,740	42 (A)
Steel	45,000	56,600	56,000	600 (F)
Other direct materials	450	566	700	134 (A)
Direct labour	29,000	35,380	32,400	2,980 (F)
Production overheads	30,000	38,430	42,600	4,170 (A)
Totals	105,800	132,674	133,440	766

Budgeting and
Performance
Evaluation

Budgeting and Performance Evaluation

13

The key metrics used in performance evaluation are

- The income statement
  - Revenue
  - Profitability
- Return on capital employed
- Asset turnover
- Liquidity

Profitability

Measures include

- Gross profit margin: Gross profit/Revenue
- Operating profit margin: Operating profit/Revenue
- Expense ratios e.g. Advertising cost/Sales, Telephone cost/Sales

The main aim of a company, this links well to corporate goals.
Targets can be net profit margin, gross profit margin, return on investment and residual income.

There may be conflict between the long and short term.

Return on capital employed (ROCE)/Return on Investment (ROI)

Operating profit/Capital employed

Asset turnover

An indicator of asset efficiency or corporate strategy.

- Asset turnover = Revenue/Capital employed

185

Note: Return on investment = Asset turnover × Net profit margin.

The efficiency with which individual components of assets are being used can also be considered:

- Inventory days = (Inventory held/Purchases) × 365
- Receivables days = (Receivables balance/Sales) × 365

Note: Liability turnover − Payables days = (Payables balance/Purchases) × 365

Liquidity

Usually viewed as an indicator of corporate survival.

Targets can be current ratio, quick ratio or individual working capital ratios such as receivables days.

- Current (liquidity) ratio = Current assets/Current liabilities
- Acid test (quick) ratio = (Cash + receivables)/Current liabilities
- Cash conversion period = Inventory days + receivables days − payables days

Reporting performance evaluation

Evaluation can either be

- Horizontal – line by line comparison of one set of data with another
- Trend – horizontal analysis extended over several years
- Vertical – expressing the data as a percentage of a critical component of the financial statements

Non-financial performance indicators

To obtain a full evaluation of performance it will also be necessary to use non-financial performance indicators (NFPIs) such as:

- Competitiveness
- Activity level
- Productivity
- Quality of service
- Customer satisfaction
- Quality of staff experience
- Innovation.

Benchmarking

Benchmarking involves setting performance targets (e.g. standards) for a business unit, based on the actual performance achieved by someone external. It can be used for financial or non-financial performance.

Clearly this will lead to targets that are hard but achievable.

Competitive benchmarking

Targets are based on the best company in a particular industry. Unfortunately data may not be easy to obtain, and even then it may not be comparable.

Internal benchmarking

The best performing division in a company is used as a target for the other divisions. This can lead to inter-divisional rivalry and conflict within the company.

Functional benchmarking

Particular business functions are compared (e.g. credit control), this is often across industries. The level of detail required can be particularly hard to obtain and the environmental conditions may be quite different.

Strategic benchmarking

Strategic methods and processes are observed in successful companies, appropriate lessons are learned and improvements implemented. This approach is clearly more general than the others and leads to less-specific improvements.

Balanced scorecard

Aims to look at both the indicators of success and determinants of future success. It looks at four 'perspectives'. Under each, a company should state its aims and specify measures of performance.

Some examples:

	Aims	*Measures**
1 Financial perspective	Profitability	ROI
	Survival	Current ratio
2 Customer perspective	Satisfaction	Returning customers
	Quality	Defect rate
3 Internal business perspective	Staff motivation	Absenteeism
	Efficiency	Throughput rates
4 Innovation and learning perspective	New products	Income from new products
	Learning	Employee suggestions adopted

* It is generally considered best practice to use ratios rather than absolute figures.

? Questions

13.1 A service company evaluates its performance using a number of key ratios. This includes the current ratio which is targeted not to fall below a value of 2.

Forecasts to date predict that receivables will fluctuate between £135,000 and £142,000, and payables between £17,000 and £22,000. The company has no inventory.

What is the maximum budgeted overdraft permitted if the company is to achieve its target?

(2 marks)

13.2 A division has a return on investment of 18% and an asset turnover of two times.

What is the division's net profit margin?

(2 marks)

13.3 A company evaluates its performance using a number of key ratios. This includes the current ratio which is targeted not to fall below a value of 1.7.

Forecasts for the elements of working capital are inventory £14,800, receivables £19,600 and payables £144,000.

What is the minimum budgeted bank balance permitted if the company is to achieve its target?

(2 marks)

13.4 A division has a net profit margin of 16% and an asset turnover of 0.9 times.

What is the division's return on investment?

(2 marks)

13.5 A company has an asset turnover of 5 and a net profit margin of 4%. It has profits of £80,000. What is the value of its capital employed?

13.6 The manager of a division has been charged with making his division more innovative. Suggest three ways in which his performance may be evaluated.

(3 marks)

13.7 Explain the balanced scorecard approach to performance evaluation.

(5 marks)

13.8 You have been asked to comment on the financial position of DB Holdings Ltd. You have obtained copies of the two most recent sets of the company's audited accounts which are summarised as follows:

All figures in £'000	2007	2008
Equipment net of depreciation	2,400	2,200
Premises	1,600	900
Inventory	560	1,080
Receivables	320	980
Cash/(Overdraft)	160	−180
Payables	−280	−780
Net Assets	4,760	4,200

Share Capital	1,600	1,600
Loan from Directors	2,200	1,400
Cumulative Retained Profits	960	1,200
Capital	4,760	4,200
Revenue (Sales)	4,800	5,800
Operating Profit	320	420
Dividends Paid	80	180

You know that due to the nature of the company's business, most of its business costs are purchases.

The chairman of DB Holdings has recently quoted in the press:

DB Holdings has always been a profitable company. However, we are following a high growth strategy and this has put pressure on cash flow. We have a number of new clients signed up and believe the future is bright.

Requirements

(a) Calculate the following business metrics for DB Holdings Ltd. in 2007 and 2008
  - ROCE
  - Profit margin on sales
  - Liquidity (or current) ratio
  - Receivables days
  - Inventory days
  - Payables days
  - Cash conversion period **(14 marks)**

(b) Critically appraise the chairman's quote and determine whether in your opinion DB Holdings Ltd. are creditworthy. **(6 marks)**

(20 marks)

✅ Answers

13.1 The ratio is at its lowest when debtors are low and creditors high.

Thus the debtors (£135,000) must be double the combined overdraft and creditors (i.e. £67,500).

O/d = £67,500 − £22,000 = £45,500.

Or using algebra:

135,000 = 2(22,000 + o/d)
 67,500 = 22,000 + o/d
  o/d = 45,500.

13.2 You need to know the relationship between these ratios.

Return on investment = net profit margin × asset turnover

Thus

Net profit margin = return on investment ÷ asset turnover
      = 18% ÷ 2
      = 9%.

13.3 Remember that the current ratio is current assets ÷ current liabilities.

Here the only liabilities seem to be creditors = £144,000

Current assets must be $1.7 \times 144,000 = 244,800$

Bank must be $244,800 - 14,800 - 19,600 = 210,400$.

13.4 You need to know the relationship between these ratios.

$$\text{Return on investment} = \text{net profit margin} \times \text{asset turnover}$$
$$= 16\% \times 0.9$$
$$= 14.4\%.$$

13.5 Return on investment = Asset turnover × Net profit margin.

Therefore ROI = $5 \times 4\% = 20\%$

ROI also = Operating profit/Capital employed

$$0.2 = \frac{£80,000}{x}$$

$x = £400,000$

13.6 Number of new products or services brought to market
Technical lead relative to competitors
Lead time to bring new products to market

13.7 The balanced scorecard approach is a way of providing information to management which involves the inclusion of non-financial information alongside financial information.

It emphasises the need to provide the user with a set of information which addresses all relevant areas of performance in an objective and unbiased fashion.

Although the specific measures used may vary, a scorecard would normally include the following measures

- profitability – the financial perspective
- customer satisfaction – the customer perspective
- innovation – the innovation and learning perspective
- internal efficiency – the internal business perspective.

By providing all this information in a single report, management is able to assess the impact of particular actions on all perspectives of the company's activities.

13.8 (a) DB Holdings Ltd. – key business metrics

	2007	2008
ROCE (Operating profit / Capital employed)	6.72	10.00
Operating profit margin (Operating profit / Revenue)	6.67	7.24
Current liquidity ratio (Current assets / Current liabilities)	3.7	2.1*
Receivables days (Receivable / Sales)	24	62
Inventory days (Inventory / Purchases**)	46	73
Payable days (Payables / Purchases**)	23	53
Cash conversion period (Inventory days + receivables days − payables days)	47	82

*Note that the overdraft in 2008 means that the company liabilities amount to 180 + 780 = 960

**Approximated as Sales – Operating profit

Note that

- In certain cases an approximate figure is used. For example, in calculating inventory days and payables days one needs to know 'purchases' – but since this is unavailable, operating costs are used instead.

  Operating costs = Sales – Operating profit.

  Since most business costs are purchases, the resultant inventory and payables days figures are meaningful and allow a clear inter-period comparison.

- Inventory and payables days positions for 2008 are both based on year end figures. Ideally we would base these figures on an average of end 2007 and end 2008 balances. However, these figures are not available, and year end figures are deemed a suitable approximation.

(b) The performance of this business appears to have been both respectable and improving having regard to both ROCE and profit margin. Those are the key performance metrics, but they do not tell the whole story. The asset turnover and liquidity position of the business has changed in a manner that should prompt some serious questions:

- Inventory days has risen dramatically. Why has this happened? Does the extra inventory really exist and how has it been valued?
- Receivables days has risen dramatically. Why has this happened? Do the extra receivables actually exist and what is the chance of bad debts arising?
- Payables days has risen dramatically. Why has this happened? Are suppliers continuing to make deliveries as normal?

That apart, there is clear evidence of assets being stripped out of the business by its owners. Property has been sold, a director loan partly repaid and dividends have been increased. These may not impact immediately on the key performance metrics – which are essentially 'backward looking' measures reporting only what has happened over a short period in the immediate past. But what is happening suggests a clear lack of commitment on the part of its directors that might impact on performance in the longer term.

To form a fuller evaluation of performance one would need to obtain a range of forward looking indicators – linked to things like market share, quality of service, response time to customer orders, proportion of customer repeat business being achieved, staff turnover and relationships with suppliers.

14

Responsibility Centres and Transfer Pricing

Responsibility Centres and Transfer Pricing

14

Return on investment (ROI)

Calculation

$$ROI = \frac{ProfitBeforeInterestAndTax}{CapitalEmployed}$$

This will be compared with a target, usually a company's cost of capital or an industry benchmark.

There are problems with all the three figures needed.

1 Profit

- Before tax?
- Accounting policies?
- Sharing of jointly made profits?
- Transfer pricing?

2 Capital

- Depreciate assets?
- Inflate assets?
- Capitalise leased assets?
- Shared assets?

3 Target

- Cost of capital (a cash-based measure)?
- Industry target (achievable, company differences)?

In addition return on investment can lead to dysfunctional decisions where the return on an investment is between the division's existing return and the target.

Example

Divisional existing return = 15%
Target return = 12%
New investment return = 14%

The manager will tend to reject since the investment would drag down the division's overall return and make the manager's performance appear worse. The company wants this investment to be undertaken since it offers a return in excess of target.

Residual income (RI)

Calculation

RI = Profit Before Interest and Tax − Target Return × Capital Employed

For good performance this is positive.

Most of the problems are the same as for return on investment, except that dysfunctional decisions should not occur.

Unfortunately residual income is not comparable between divisions (it is in £ not %).

Transfer pricing

A transfer price (TP) is an internal price used to record sales from one division to another. It splits corporate profit between the divisions.

Aims

- Goal congruence between divisions and company
- Incentives to managers to produce
- Good performance evaluation
- Divisional autonomy
- Equitable profit split.

In practice no transfer price will achieve all these aims.

Methods

Cost plus. Transfer price is set at cost plus a profit margin (NB standard cost is better than actual, marginal cost usually better than absorption cost).

Two part. Transfer price is a unit charge (usually based on marginal cost) plus a periodic charge (usually based on fixed overheads).

Negotiated. The divisions agree a transfer price between themselves.

Market. Use the open market price for the transferred good (sometimes modified by divisional cost savings).

Dual price. The selling division has a different price to the purchasing division (usually absorption cost + mark-up and marginal cost respectively).

Optimum transfer pricing

About the best TP can be found using the following (assuming A sells to B):

Division A   TP > marginal cost + opportunity cost (zero, if spare capacity)

Division B   TP < unit contribution (before transfer price) and

                TP < external price

International transfer pricing

The transfer price can be used to move profits around to minimise global tax liabilities and to repatriate profits, circumventing some currency controls.

❓ Questions

14.1 Distinguish between profit and investment centres and explain the link to the concept of decentralisation.

(5 marks)

14.2 A company has set a target ROI of 12% for its divisions, this is deemed to represent the return necessary to benefit the company.

Division D achieved an ROI of 17% last year and is not expecting any major change from ongoing operations.

The purchase of a new piece of equipment has been proposed by a member of the production team. It is estimated that it will boost profits by £128,000 per annum for an investment of £855,000.

Is the divisional manager likely to accept or reject the investment? Will this be to the benefit or the detriment of the company?

14.3 A company has set a target ROI of 14% for its divisions, this is based on the company's cost of capital.

Division D achieved an ROI of 8% last year and is not expecting any major change from ongoing operations. However, a manager has suggested that cost savings of £15,000 per annum can be obtained by investing £135,000 in upgrading a particular piece of equipment.

Is the divisional manager likely to accept or reject the investment? Will this be to the benefit or the detriment of the company?

14.4 A company uses ROI to assess divisional performance, but it is considering switching to RI. The company's cost of capital is 15%.

Division C has an ROI of 21% which is not expected to change. An investment of £155,000 is available, which is expected to yield profits of £28,000 per annum.

Is the manager of division C likely to accept or reject the investment if ROI is used to assess performance? Would this change if RI was used?

(2 marks)

14.5 Division G of a large company is approaching its year end. The division is evaluated using ROI with a target rate of return of 15%. The division has control of all aspects of its operation except that all cash balances are centralised by the company and therefore left off divisional balance sheets.

The divisional manager is considering the following options.

(i) To delay payment of a supplier until next year, the potential prompt payment discount of 5% will be lost. The debt is for £27,500.

(ii) To scrap a redundant asset with a book value of £147,000. The manager has been offered £15,000 as immediate scrap proceeds, whilst he is fairly confident that he could get £25,000 in an industry auction to be held at the start of the new year.

Assume that the manager is very short-termist (i.e. only considers the implications for this year) and that the expected ROI for the year, before these options, is 18%.

Which of the following represents the most likely combination that the manager will choose?

	(i)	(ii)
A	Delay	Scrap now
B	Delay	Scrap next year
C	Do not delay	Scrap now
D	Do not delay	Scrap next year

(2 marks)

14.6 A divisionalised company uses transfer pricing as part of its management information system. Each manager is assessed on their divisional profit.

Division A makes a unit for £10 variable cost and £3 of fixed cost is absorbed.
Division B takes these units, incurs another £8 variable cost and absorbs £4.
It then sells them for £21.
The transfer price is set at £12.

There are no capacity constraints and all fixed costs are unavoidable in the short run.

(4 marks)

Determine whether each of the managers of divisions A and B are likely to produce the units. From the company's perspective, should production occur and is the transfer price goal congruent?

14.7   Which of the following is NOT a method of transfer pricing?

A   Cost plus transfer price
B   Internal price transfer price
C   Market-based transfer price
D   Two part transfer price.

(2 marks)

Use the following information to answer the next two questions.

Division A of a company makes units which are then transferred to other divisions.

There is a competitive intermediate market for these units, with a price of £15 per unit. Division A then incurs a selling cost of £2.
Variable production cost = £7 per unit and fixed cost = £3 per unit.

14.8   Assume the division has spare capacity.

What is the minimum TP that will encourage the divisional manager of A to transfer units to other divisions?

(2 marks)

14.9   Assume the division has no spare capacity.

What is the minimum TP that will encourage the divisional manager of A to transfer units to other divisions?

(2 marks)

14.10   TM plc makes components which it sells internally to its subsidiary RM Ltd, as well as to its own external market.

The external market price is £24.00 per unit, which yields a contribution of 40% of sales. For external sales, variable costs include £1.50 per unit for distribution costs, which are not incurred on internal sales.

TM plc has sufficient capacity to meet all of the internal and external sales. In order to maximise group profit, at what unit price should the component be transferred to RM Ltd?

(2 marks)

14.11   Division A makes alphas which are converted into betas by division B. A's variable costs are £150 per unit and B's are £80 per unit. B sells completed betas for £290 each.

There is an intermediate market for alphas with a price of £180 which significantly exceeds the capacity of divisions A and B.

(i)   Assuming that B cannot buy from the market in alphas (but A can sell into the market), what is the widest range of TP that encourages the divisions to trade with each other?

(ii)   Assuming that A cannot sell into the market in alphas (but B can buy from the market), what is the widest range of TP that now encourages the divisions to trade with each other?

(5 marks)

14.12   XYZ motor group comprises three autonomous divisions and its divisional managers are paid salary bonuses linked to the profit that their respective divisions achieve.

The New Vehicle (NV) division has a city showroom. It sells new vehicles and accepts trade-ins which are sold to the Used Vehicle (UV) division at a 'going trade price' less any necessary repair costs. The Vehicle Repair (VR) division performs necessary repair work to trade-ins and invoices UV for such work on a full cost plus basis. Both the UV and VR divisions do a great deal of business unrelated to trade-ins.

NV has the option of selling a new vehicle to a customer for £40,000 (including a 25% profit mark up on cost) providing the customer is given a trade-in value of £28,000 on his old vehicle. Reference to used car value guides indicate that the going trade price for the trade-in vehicle will be £17,500. However, it is estimated that UV division will be able to sell the trade in for £28,900 after incurring a charge from VR for repairing the vehicle as follows:

	£
Variable costs	500
Fixed overheads	250 (being 50% of VCs)
Mark up	75 (being 10% on cost)
Total	825

Requirements

(a) Calculate the impact on the contribution of each division and XYZ in total of proceeding with the new car sale on the terms specified

(10 marks)

(b) Explain the possible sources of conflict between the managers of the three divisions and the XYZ group management arising from the organisational arrangement of the XYZ group and its transfer pricing system

(8 marks)

(c) Having regard to your answers to (a) and (b) propose any modifications to the transfer pricing system that your consider appropriate

(7 marks)

Note: the 'trade price' for a used vehicle is the price at which one car dealer would sell a vehicle to another dealer without warranties or guarantees

(Total = 25 marks)

✓ Answers

14.1　A profit centre exists where a manager is responsible for both costs and revenues in their divisions. An investment centre exists where a manager is responsible for costs, revenues and the acquisition and disposal of the assets used to support the divisions' activities.

Decentralisation in an organisation, refers to the degree of authority delegated by top management to lower level operating management. At one end of the spectrum, where complete executive control over activities is maintained by head office, and all decisions are made at the top level, the organisation is totally *centralised*. At the other end, where the degree of autonomy exercised by lower level managers gives them full control over activities and decisions, it would be described as totally *decentralised*.

An organisation operating investment centres is likely to be described as decentralised. One operating profit centres would be seen as somewhere in the middle of the spectrum.

14.2　The ROI of the investment is £128,000 ÷ £855,000 = 15%.

Thus the manager's performance will appear to decline if he takes on this project (his new return will fall below the existing 17%). He will therefore reject this investment.

However, a return of 15% is beneficial to the company, and so the manager rejects to the detriment of the company.

14.3　The ROI of the investment is £15,000 ÷ £135,000 = 11%.

Thus the manager's performance will appear to improve if he takes on this project (his new return will rise above the existing 8%). He will therefore accept this investment.

However, a return of 11% is detrimental to the company, and so the manager accepts to the detriment of the company.

14.4   The ROI of the investment is £28,000 ÷ £155,000 = 18%.

This will reduce the division's ROI and will cause the manager to reject.

The RI is £28,000 − 15% × £155,000 = £4,750.

Since this is positive the manager will accept.

14.5   **A**

It is worth noting that you do not need the figures to work this question out (although you can use them if you want).

(i)   Paying now would reduce creditors and thus increase capital employed, leading to lower rates of return. Note that the "return" of 5% is nowhere near high enough to make this worth considering.

(ii)   Scrapping will reduce the capital employed, leading to higher returns, the income will just accentuate this.

14.6   Each manager will only consider costs that are variable to him, fixed costs will be ignored – they are unavoidable.

Manager A will want to produce as the transfer price (£12) exceeds his variable cost (£10), adding to his contribution.

Manager B will want to produce as the revenue from the sale (£21) exceeds the variable cost and transfer price (£8 + £12), adding to his contribution.

The company will increase its contribution if production occurs, because the final selling price is greater than the total variable costs.

The position is goal congruent since both divisions wish to produce.

14.7   **B**

The internal price is just another name for the TP, so it is not a method of transfer pricing.

14.8   Any price above variable cost will generate a positive contribution, and will therefore be accepted.

14.9   The division will need to give up a unit sold externally in order to make a transfer, this is only worthwhile if the income of a transfer is greater than the *net* income of an external sale.

14.10   You must set a price high enough for TM to cover its costs, but not so high that RM cannot make a profit.

For TM, an item sold externally has VC of 60% × £24.00 = £14.40

Of this, £1.50 will not be incurred on an internal transfer so it is not relevant here, VC on internal transfer = £14.40 − £1.50 = £12.90

We do not know RM's cost structure, so we leave the price at £12.90; this will ensure that RM is not discouraged from taking an internal transfer when it is profitable to do so.

14.11 (i) A can sell all of its output into the intermediate market at £180, so the TP needs to exceed this.

B needs to make a contribution so the TP needs to be below £290 − £80 = £210

So, £180 < TP < £210.

(ii) A needs to cover its costs, so TP must exceed £150.

B can buy from the intermediate market at £180, so the TP must be lower than this.

So, £150 < TP < £180.

14.12 (a)

NV (New Vehicle division)

	£
Margin on new vehicle	8,000 (40,000 × 20%)
Trade in value given	−28,000
Transfer price	−16,675 (17,500 − 825)
Total	−3,325

UV (Used Vehicle division)

	£
Sale proceeds	28,900
Repair costs	−825
Transfer price	−16,675
Total	11,400

VR (Vehicle Repair division)

	£
Repairs invoiced	825
Variable costs	−500
Total	325

XYZ Motor Group

	£
NV	−3,325
UV	11,400
VR	325
Total	8,400

(b) Sources of conflict may possibly include any or all of the following:

- The existing system places all the benefit from the sale of used cars with UV division. In the absence of trade-ins this might be fair, but obtaining used cars as trade-ins on sale of new cars involves input from NV division. It would be equitable to allow a margin to NV division on such transactions.
- In the case study given, the decision on whether or not to accept the deal on the sale of the new £40,000 car rests with the NV division manager.

Although the deal is profitable to the XYZ group, the transfer price system means that it inflicts a small loss on NV. The NV manager might turn it down.

- The system allows VR division to pass on to NV all its costs plus a generous margin for the work it does. This might encourage VR division to load costs onto transfer work and to pass on inefficiencies to other divisions.
- VR's transfer charges include both fixed and variable components with no allowance for the existence or otherwise of opportunity costs. Although not critical in the case study, such a situation may induce sub-optimal decision making when NV or UV division perceives all of the VR's charges to be fixed.

(c) The ideal or correct transfer price is the marginal cost incurred by the transferor division plus any opportunity cost suffered by that division. This (1) provides a reasonably equitable distribution of profit between the transferor and transferee division and (2) minimises the possibility of dysfunctional behaviour. However, it can be very difficult to design and operate a system that works on this principle.

One difficulty is that it can be difficult to state unambiguously what marginal cost is. The marginal cost of doing something may be different when viewed on a short-term or long-term basis. Furthermore, opportunity cost may be a very vague concept. If VR is not working to full capacity then a £500 marginal cost for the job might be a fair transfer price. But if VR is working to full capacity and has to turn away outside work offering a contribution of £325 then £825 becomes a fair transfer price for the job in question. But whether or not VR is working to full capacity at any given time may be difficult to determine with certainty. In any event, it may be possible to defer outside work rather than turn it away in order to free up some capacity. It is difficult to accommodate such an imprecise state of affairs in a structured system.

The internal transfer of used vehicles to UV division at trade price appears to be inequitable. Given NV'S contribution to the acquisition it seems fairer that the used cars be transferred at trade price plus a mark up. This would allow for the fact that many of the activities and risks normally associated with the outside purchase of a used car are avoided by UV in the case of internal transfers.

A simple and practical solution to the problems of XYZ might include the following principal system design features:

- Transfer of trade-in vehicles from NV to UV at trade price plus a mark up. The mark up should recognize the role that NV plays in obtaining the trade-in.
- Charging the cost of VR repairs to NV and UV at marginal cost plus a modest margin – unless there is a clear capacity shortage. Alternatively, VR might be required to quote for transfer work against outside competitors.

Exam Q & As

At the time of publication there are no exam Q & As available for the 2010 syllabus. However, the latest specimen exam papers are available on the CIMA website. Actual exam Q & As will be available free of charge to CIMA students on the CIMA website from summer 2010 onwards.

BRISBANE

Photography by Eric Taylor • Text by Des Partridge

BRISBANE

HODDER & STOUGHTON AUSTRALIA

First published in 1991
by Hodder & Stoughton (Australia) Pty Limited,
10-16 South Street, Rydalmere, NSW, 2116.

National Library of Australia Cataloguing-in-Publication entry

Taylor, Eric, 1952–
    Brisbane.

    ISBN 0 340 54121 0.

    1. Brisbane (Qld.) — Description — 1976–   — Views.
    I. Partridge, Des, 1940–   II. Title.

994.310630222

Designed and typeset by Concept Communications Pty Ltd
Printed in Hong Kong

Introduction

Brisbane is my home; what's more it is my favourite city. Brisbane is part of me, the background to my life. It has been a delight to see more and more people appreciate its beauty and distinctive lifestyle. It is also a delight to share in this visual tribute to its special character from a distinguished photographer.

In the period leading up to Australia's bicentennial year I discovered that the Partridge family connection goes back about 150 years. My great-great-grandfather George Partridge settled in the area sometime in the 1840s. He arrived in New South Wales in 1833 as an eighteen year old convict, sentenced to seven years for the offence of pick-pocketing in his native Birmingham. After serving his time, George somehow drifted to the Moreton Bay area. James Peardon had arrived in Sydney as a convict at the same time as George and settled at Drayton near Toowoomba. In 1850, George married Mary Peardon, James's daughter in St John's church, Brisbane — soon to be St John's Cathedral. When he died, aged sixty-eight, George was living in Margaret Street, Brisbane, and the records show that he was buried in Toowong Cemetery, just a few kilometres from where we now live. We have not been able to find his grave and pay our respects to my convict ancestor, but perhaps this book is a kind of tribute to him and many others who have been part of Brisbane's history.

Today, the convict past is barely in evidence, although the remnants that remain are prized as precious links with the past. The Commissariat Store and the Wickham Terrace windmill, both constructed in 1829 are the oldest buildings, while Newstead House, constructed in 1846 and home of the Government Resident until separation, is the city's oldest surviving residence.

When I was a youngster in the 1950s Brisbane was a city with pavements protected from sun and rain by distinctive awnings. These and the verandas on houses and public buildings emphasised the city's tropical setting. The designs were in harmony with the environment.

Brisbane of the 90s has become a city of high-rise concrete and glass towers, many of striking design, but as a result the city's individual flavour is fast vanishing, replaced by a glossy internationalism.

What has been exciting about central Brisbane's recent development though, has been its rediscovery of the Brisbane River (discovered and named by John Oxley in 1823 while looking for a site for the Moreton Bay penal settlement) which was Brisbane's starting point. Later city developers turned their back on the river. But, these days, it has again become the focal point of the city — with space left between office towers to open up vistas to the water-front and access to its pleasures.

Brisbane has been my home town now since the early 1960s and, in my experience there is none better. Friendly, open, hospitable, it fulfils all the promise of the tourist brochures. In this case, they are true. It is growing alarmingly fast, around 1.2 million now and rising, and modern big-city pressures are more acute, but it's still a place in which everybody can be rich in enjoyment. With an abundance of parks and gardens, festivals, sporting venues, art galleries, libraries; the proximity of national parks and beaches; backyards in which to laze and do nothing — you don't have to be a millionaire to enjoy this lifestyle. Life in Brisbane has also acquired a distinctly multi-cultural flavour — the more than 150 ethnic groups represented in the population add immensely to its vitality.

The brilliant light of Brisbane — so bright it can hurt if you forget your sunglasses — is a constant surprise to newcomers, and a delight to photographers.

Des Partridge

I first came to Brisbane to photograph the city in preparation for an exhibition celebrating its becoming a sister city of Auckland. I had the advantage then of seeing Brisbane through the eyes of a stranger.

My photography is based on an awareness of light, its fleeting rhythms and patterns, and that project gave me all the scope I needed to explore them from moment to moment. The golden light of dawn reflected, through early morning mist, on the city's mirror high rise, the grey threat of violent afternoon thunderstorms, the rainforests of the hinterland — it all felt familiar yet so different and exotic.

That initial collection of photographs has slowly expanded to form the basis of this book. It is a tribute to the city which is now my home.

Eric Taylor

OVERLEAF From its settlement in 1825 as a penal settlement for around 1,000 convicts guarded by fewer than 200 soldiers Brisbane has grown into a bustling city with a population of 1.2 million. The penal settlement had only a ten-year life, and few traces of it remain. Here the early morning light picks up the winding course of the river from the city eastward to the sea.

PREVIOUS PAGE Multi-storey office towers now dress the city in the international uniform of success, the outward sign of prosperity and confidence in its future. Modern developers have made the Brisbane River the focus of their buildings. In this view upriver, the suburbs spread over the city of eleven hills in all directions, and on the western horizon are the foothills of the Great Dividing Range.

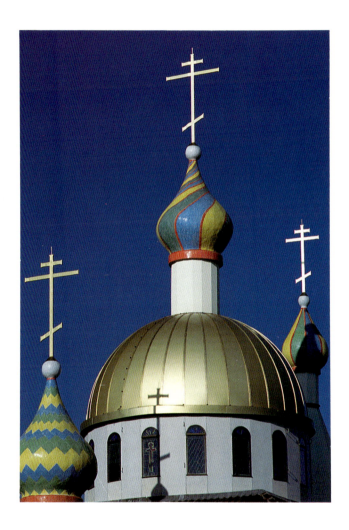

ABOVE Not St Basil's, Moscow, but Brisbane. The congregation of the Russian Orthodox Church, Rocklea, built their church in the traditional style as a reminder of home.

OPPOSITE Small boats moored at the Botanical Gardens reach of the Brisbane River are dwarfed by the shiny towers of the financial centre. The 39-storey office block of the Waterfront Place development dominates the scene and the dome of the nineteenth century Customs House on the extreme right, reminds us that Brisbane has always been a river port.

ABOVE The undisputed Queen of the Brisbane River, the paddlewheeler Kookaburra Queen II, waits at the Pier, Waterfront Place, for its next river trip to begin. A replica of nineteenth century Mississippi River paddlewheelers, the Kookaburra Queen went into service on the eve of World Expo 1988.

Mr Gary Balkin introduced paddlewheelers to the Brisbane River in April 1986, with his larger Kookaburra Queen. The thirty metre luxury vessel was built of local and imported timbers and powered by diesel engines. It was such a success with locals and visitors alike that he commissioned a second paddlewheeler to cater for the influx of Expo visitors.

The Kookaburra Queens were built in Brisbane at Bulimba, just down river from the city centre and are the only wooden paddlewheelers to be built in Australia this century.

The original Kookaburra Queen is, these days, based on the Gold Coast, where it has become one of the most popular attractions. The Kookaburra II serves Brisbane, and is in great demand for special functions and tourist trips.

As well as the Pier berth, the Waterfront Place development provides a number of quality riverside restaurants and tourist shops.

OPPOSITE Early morning commuter ferry approaching Waterfront Place.

BELOW Five bridges cross the Brisbane River's city reach. Here, looking up river towards Milton; an arch of the William Jolly bridge combines with that of the Merivale Railway Bridge, opened in November 1979, to make a striking composition.

The railway bridge connects the South Brisbane and Roma Street railway stations and is 1,200 metres long. Its elegant bowstring arch rises to 132 metres at its highest point. The neighbouring William Jolly Bridge — originally called simply the 'Grey Street Bridge' — was opened in 1932.

OPPOSITE The cupola on the tower of the Brisbane Polo Club's building (formerly Naldham House) hints of Brisbane's colonial past, and, behind it, the twentieth century high-rise buildings are reflected in the glass surface of the striking Waterfront Place tower. Naldham House was built in 1889 for the Australian United Steam Navigation Company. The building has recently been taken over by the Polo Club as its headquarters. For its 1,500 members — who pay a joining fee of $5,000 each — two floors of the former shipping building underwent a 2.5 million dollar refurbishment to provide bar, lounge and dining-room facilities.

The club's polo fields are at leafy Fig Tree Pocket in the city's western suburbs.

LEFT Another day, another peak hour on the Riverside Expressway which carries traffic between the city and the southern suburbs. It continues south and east towards the Gold Coast.

This expressway, the striking Captain Cook bridge and south-east freeway were recommended to the State Government and Brisbane City Council by an American firm of consultants following an extensive transportation study in 1965. Construction began in 1968, and did not finish until the Logan Road–Springwood section of the freeway was completed in late 1985.

The Captain Cook section of the expressway carries Queensland's heaviest traffic flow, somewhere in excess of 100,000 vehicles daily. It is one of the busiest roadways in Australia. To keep pace with the ever-increasing traffic, the bridge is being extended to provide four lanes inbound and outbound.

BELOW Two students of St Laurence's College in South Brisbane face up to another school day. The college, established in 1915, is known as 'The School on the Hill'. Its position gives it a prized view over the city, even in this city of many hills and many schools — state, church and independent — at primary and secondary level. These and its many tertiary institutions draw students from all over Queensland and overseas, particularly from Asia.

OPPOSITE Morning in the inner-city suburb of New Farm and one of the 'lollipop' attendants is on duty to protect primary school children at a busy roadcrossing. The State Transport Department employs more than 1300 attendants — on duty each morning and afternoon — at some 653 school crossings from Weipa in the far north to the New South Wales border.

BELOW Brisbane houses of yesterday were distinctive, not only because they were made of wood, with corrugated iron roofs but, because they were built on stilts — or stumps as Queenslanders call them. These houses, in the north-western suburb of Red Hill, have their backs perched on extremely high stumps, mainly to keep the front door level with the street.

OPPOSITE The old and the new, the spire of the late nineteenth century St Paul's Presbyterian Church in Spring Hill reflected in the glass facade of the office tower next door. The glorious sandstone building was designed by one of Brisbane's most illustrious early architects, F.D.G. Stanley, the designer of the General Post Office building, the Queen Street branch of the National Bank — now the National Australia Bank — the Harbours and Marine buildings and the Queensland Club.

St Paul's original congregation was formed by the families of Scottish Presbyterians who arrived in Brisbane on the *Fortitude* in 1849. Presbyterian clergyman the Reverend Dr John Dunmore Lang, promoter and journalist, had organised three ships to carry about six hundred new settlers to the infant Brisbane. The other two ships were the *Chaseley* and the *Lima*.

The congregation of St Paul's was founded in 1863, and the foundation stone of the sandstone building was laid in 1887.

19

The first section of the Queen Street Mall was opened in 1982, the year that Brisbane played host for the Commonwealth Games. It became so popular that it was extended in 1988 in time for the World Expo. It now spans Queen Street for the length of two city blocks. A pedestrian mall for Brisbane had been part of the original town plan provided for Governor Gipps by surveyors he sent from Sydney in 1839. Their instructions included provision of pedestrian-only avenues and extensive squares. However, after visiting the place, Governor Gipps seems to have decided that Brisbane would never be much of a town, and the plan was cancelled. If he came back now, he might be more impressed.

ABOVE The Mall features licensed buskers — such as these members of the Brisbane Subway Band — who give performances throughout the day and into the night. The band leader here is accordion player, Colin Loise. Another well known member is squeeze-box player John Eames — who is eighty-three — and the band's conductor is Molly Dunne. Molly celebrated her ninetieth birthday in 1990.

OPPOSITE Two children from different backgrounds pause in the Mall to enjoy ice-creams together.

ABOVE A New Farm resident heads for home after a
shopping expedition.

OPPOSITE The doorstep of an Adelaide Street chemist
provides a convenient spot to wait for the bus.

ABOVE Brisbane's imposing City Hall was opened in 1930. One of its most striking features is the sculptured tympanum over the main King George Square entrance which is supported by eight majestic Corinthian columns. The relief figures are the work of acclaimed Brisbane sculptor Daphne Mayo and are, of course, allegorical. The central figure represents the State protecting the citizens, the left-hand side the arrival of the Europeans and the right-hand side the early white explorers.

OPPOSITE Although buildings in a variety of architectural styles surround the General Post Office in Queen Street, it remains one of Brisbane's most distinctive nineteenth century buildings — much enhanced by the recently cleared and landscaped Post Office Square opposite. The General Post Office and Central Station — two old sandstone buildings — face each other along the axis formed by Post Office Square and Anzac Square.

Behind the Post Office can be seen the spires and roofline of St Stephen's Roman Catholic Cathedral.

BELOW Ready for the greens, a group of lawn bowlers wait for transport. More than 82,000 people belong to the two associations that organise and control the sport in Queensland — the Queensland Ladies' Bowling Association has 27,544 members and the men's Royal Queensland Bowling Association, 54,980. There are 360 bowling clubs in the State, making lawn bowls — which is played all-year-round — Queenland's most popular sport. Bowling has begun to attract younger and younger players, and competitions are now organised for players under eighteen.

Women have played the sport in Queensland since the early 1920s; the QLBA, celebrated its diamond jubilee in 1990.

OPPOSITE Under the deep shade of Moreton Bay fig trees a BMX is raffled to raise funds for the Sacred Heart Primary School, Sandgate.

RIGHT Brisbane dramatically highlighted against a late afternoon storm cloud. The city, once regarded by visitors as sleepy, has taken on a new vitality in the past ten years. Big events such as the Commonwealth Games (1982) and World Expo (1988) drew thousands of people to the Queensland capital to visit and many to stay. A boom in high-rise office accommodation in the 80s has changed the city skyline for ever.

ABOVE The unmistakably sub-tropical atmosphere of
Brisbane is asserted by this flourishing palm tree alongside
the dizzy height of Waterfront Place and the elegant Polo
Club headquarters.

OPPOSITE Heaven can't be far from here... swirling
clouds reflected in one of the all-glass towers fashionable
with Brisbane architects and developers.

ABOVE A solemn tribute to those who did not come home
— Anzac Day at Buderim, in the hills north of Brisbane.

RIGHT An eternal flame burns in the centre of the
ANZAC Memorial in the heart of Brisbane. The bronze
urn in which the flame burns is surrounded by Doric
columns of local sandstone. Sixty thousand Queensland
men served as members of the Australia and New Zealand
Army Corps (ANZAC) in World War I. The Memorial
was dedicated to them and built on land donated by the
Federal and State Governments during the 1920s term of
the first Lord Mayor of Brisbane, William Jolly. In Anzac
Square, which the Memorial overlooks, there are
monuments to the fallen in the Boer War, World War II,
the Korean and Vietnam Wars.

Every year on Anzac Day — 25 April — here and
throughout the country ceremonies are held to honour
those who served in all wars.

BELOW The city reach of the Brisbane River is the setting for the annual raft race organised by local radio station 4BC for charity. It is a fun event for which competitors devise all sorts of zany craft. This one was entered by the State Department of Primary Industries and crewed by staff members.

OPPOSITE The sea was Brisbane's lifeline in its early days. Ships travelling to the new settlement could navigate the Brisbane River, but as ships became larger they had to anchor in Moreton Bay. Dredging began in the 1860s, allowing river wharves to operate, but port development has moved over the years to the mouth of the river at Fisherman Island.

Since 1981 this has been Brisbane's port, with the container terminal offering the most modern facilities. It is first port of call on Asian and Pacific routes, and the largest river port in Australia.

PREVIOUS PAGE These three crews represent the rowing clubs of the three Brisbane tertiary institutions — the University of Queensland, Griffith University and the multi-campuses of the Queensland University of Technology — lined up for a race which has become an annual event on the Toowong reach of the river.

ABOVE We won't take part, not this year anyway... From the quiet waters of Shorncliffe on Moreton Bay, a sailing enthusiast watches the big yachts pass at the beginning of the long haul to Gladstone, 307 nautical miles to the north.

OPPOSITE Red spinnaker catching the wind, the 30 metre yacht *Woodstock,* heads north at the start of the annual Easter Brisbane–Gladstone ocean yacht race. The first race in 1949 attracted a modest seven competitors; these days there are sixty to seventy entries each year.

PREVIOUS PAGE One small yacht in an expanse of sky and sea off the Sunshine Coast, north of Brisbane.

LEFT One of the largest marinas in the southern hemisphere — with berths for 410 craft — has been built for the Royal Queensland Yacht Squadron at its Manly headquarters. The yacht club, established in 1885, was given its 'Royal' title in 1902 by King Edward VII. The Duke and Duchess of Kent were special visitors for the club's centenary celebrations.

OVERLEAF Surfers Paradise, capital of the Gold Coast, from the air.

The Gold Coast was once a low-key holiday area for
Brisbane families with simple holiday houses and basic
accommodation. It is now the year-round playground for
Australia. Its long unbroken stretch of wide sandy beach,
equitable climate, and accommodation to suit all tastes and
pockets from low-budget to five-star luxury level bring
holiday-makers from round the world. They flock to
Surfers Paradise, the brightest spot on the resort strip,
with plenty of action on the beach by day, and in the
nightclubs after dark.

PREVIOUS PAGE One of the fastest growing water sports, combining the pleasures of sailing with the thrills of surfboard riding, is windsurfing. Main Beach, Surfers Paradise, is one of the best places to see the sleek, brightly coloured craft and skilled riders in action.

ABOVE A fragile paper kite floats skywards between the sea and the solid towers of Surfers Paradise apartment buildings.

OPPOSITE A young Japanese visitor dines under the golden arches of a McDonald's restaurant.

ABOVE Where do old panel-vans go? If it's Surfers Paradise, they can end up adding a Salvador Dali touch to local architecture. Unique roof decoration and an effective eye-catcher.

OPPOSITE No, not Florence, but Surfers Paradise. A $200,000 replica of Michelangelo's David startles shoppers in Raptis Plaza, in the heart of a city where surprise is an everyday experience. The statue was carved from a thirty-three tonne block of Carrara marble from the same quarry used for the original some five hundred years ago and is one of only two full-size replicas in the world.

The shopping centre, known for the quality of its fashion shops, also boasts giant palm trees and pools of water to suggest a cool oasis from sun and sand.

BELOW Silhouetted figures enjoy the relaxation of fishing off Dunwich, North Stradbroke Island, in Moreton Bay. The island's small permanent population is boosted by weekend and holiday visitors who travel to the island by ferry.

OVERLEAF Summer storms can be ferocious, even if short-lived, and often bring high seas to lash the coast. This dramatic scene of spray and foam was taken at Alexandra Headland.

LEFT The surfboat crew from Dicky Beach, Caloundra, heads out on a regular practice run.

Australia's surf lifesaving organisation is recognised as the best in the world. It is now extending its activities to include events like Iron Man endurance competitions involving ocean swimming, surfing, board paddling and beach running.

OVERLEAF These young visitors are specks dwarfed by the towering sandhills of Fraser Island off Hervey Bay near Maryborough. Thousands of visitors are drawn to this spectacular island, the largest in the world composed entirely of sand. It is 120km long and, at its widest point, 25km across. Its sandhills rise to a height of 240m above sea level; there are great timber forests, freshwater lakes and streams.

Wild brumbies can be found on the island and dingoes. As the latter represent the most pure strain of dingo in Australia, there is a total ban on other dogs on the island. This great island's environment has been under threat from timber logging and sand mining, but an environmentally-aware public now seems determined to preserve its unique character.

ABOVE The warning sign at Eagle Farm race track does not deter trusting race-goers from leaving their binoculars. Brisbane has a booming racing industry. Regular meetings at Eagle Farm and Doomben, and a major winter carnival draw trainers, horses and jockeys from all parts of Australia and New Zealand.

LEFT The track is wet — but that's how these beach sprinters on the shores of Moreton Bay at Sandgate like it. These 'below-sea-level' races are part of the annual Back-to-Sandgate festivities, usually held in April.

LEFT This rodeo competitor at Beenleigh south of Brisbane helps preserve the pioneer tradition of rural skills. The rodeo circuit is as busy and popular as ever, with regular events throughout the state.

Since 1876, August for Brisbane residents and many from country areas of the state has been Exhibition time. 'The Ekka', as locals know it, is a combined pastoral, agricultural and industrial show, and has always been popular. The opening day of the first show drew 17,000 when the city's entire population numbered just 22,000. It now runs for ten days on its 21.9 ha site at Bowen Hills and about 830,000 people go through its turnstiles. The Exhibition Association earned the right to call itself the Royal National Agricultural and Industrial Association in 1921. But, in Brisbane, it is 'The Ekka'.

The grand parade for the cream of the state's livestock is held on Show Wednesday, a public holiday for the metropolitan area.

ABOVE Cattle judging in progress.

OPPOSITE On parade — a champion guernsey bull and proud owner.

ABOVE Who will buy? Every child — and quite a few
adults — who visits the show takes home a soft toy or a
kewpie doll on a stick.

OPPOSITE Then there's the thrill of a ride on the giant
ferris wheel.

PREVIOUS PAGE Palm trees and backyard pools — it's not Paradise, so it must be Brisbane. The sunny climate, outdoor lifestyle and average summer temperature of about 25°C makes a backyard pool as essential to life as a barbecue area. Brisbane City Council has almost 29,000 private pools on its register.

ABOVE This gracious single-storey brick colonial house is *Eulalia* built in the southern suburb of Norman Park in 1889 for Judge Patrick Real. The Hancock family acquired the extensive property in the 1930s and have since re-created an historical village in the 2 hectare grounds. Now called Early Street, the village has examples of early Brisbane architecture including *Stromness* — more than a century old — and *Auchenflower* which was home to three former State Premiers. All of the buildings except *Eulalia* are open to the public.

OPPOSITE A colonial touch for this garden wedding party in the Early Street grounds, near the 1872 slab cottage, moved from its original site and rebuilt here where it will be preserved as part of the historical village.

ABOVE No prizes for guessing that these young rugby league fans are supporting the Brisbane Broncos with their half-time entertainment for a Broncos' home game. The local club was admitted to the New South Wales rugby league premiership competition in 1988, and has attracted an enormous following. Crowds of 20,000 and more are routine for their home games at Lang Park. For years the headquarters for Queensland Rugby League, Lang Park was in the 1830s the site of one of the colony's earliest cemeteries.

OPPOSITE Brisbane Grammar (left) and the Anglican Church Grammar School (known as 'Churchie') are traditional rugby rivals. The Greater Public Schools rugby competition, a highlight of Brisbane winter sport, involves teams from Grammar, 'Churchie', Nudgee College, Gregory Terrace, Brisbane Boys' College, Brisbane State High, Ipswich Grammar, the Southport School and Toowoomba Grammar. It has produced many players for both State and Australian teams.

PREVIOUS PAGE The fans go wild, so the Broncos have scored again.

ABOVE Not Zorba's dance this time but dancers in traditional Greek costumes showing another aspect of Brisbane's multi-culturalism at a Greek festival in South Brisbane.

OPPOSITE The Greeks have their traditional dances, so do the British. A brightly costumed Morris dancer waits for the Maypole dancing to begin.

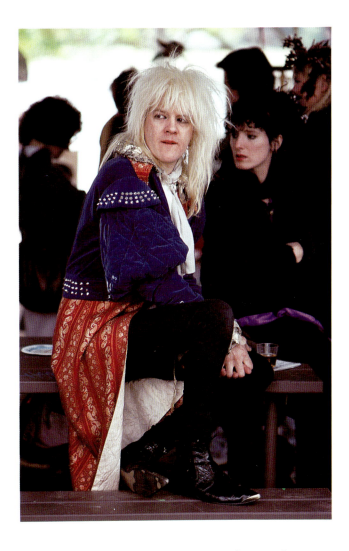

ABOVE Not typical dress for a modern sub-tropical city, but this man's elaborate and colourful costume was highly appropriate for Brisbane's Medieval Fayre. Then came the rain and it was time to take cover.

OPPOSITE Brightly coloured umbrellas fend off the raindrops at the annual Brookfield dog show in Brisbane's western suburbs.

Shades of Sir Walter Scott. The Medieval Fayre is staged annually by the Queensland Folk Federation. For this popular event enthusiasts like these wear medieval costumes. Wandering minstrels, jugglers, jesters and acrobatic acts add to the atmosphere of another era.

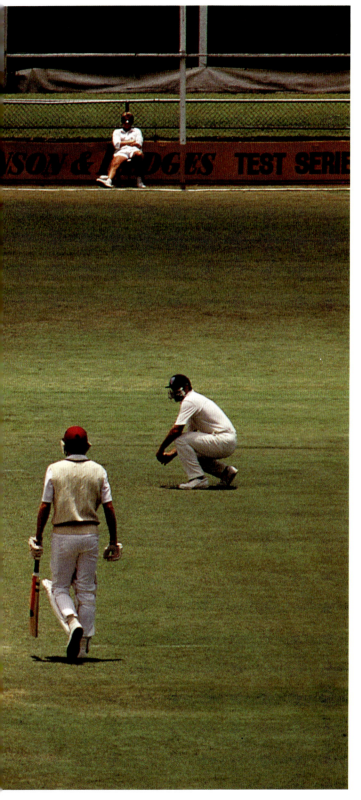

ABOVE What would Sir Donald Bradman make of this? Lunchtime entertainment at the Gabba cricket ground can involve Kanga Cricket — played on stilts with a giant bat.

LEFT Tension at the headquarters of Queensland cricket, the famed Gabba ground at Woolloongabba, south of the river and ten minutes from the city centre. Traditional rivals, Queensland (the Maroons) and New South Wales (the Blues) are involved in this match — part of the Sheffield Shield interstate series. Queensland has yet to win the Shield — the gift of the Earl of Sheffield in the 1890s — although it has played in the series since 1927.

PREVIOUS PAGE The rich red volcanic soil of 'the salad bowl of Brisbane', the Victoria Point–Redland Bay area southeast of the city. Many market gardens have, in recent years, made way for housing developments, but many remain, providing fresh vegetables, and prime strawberries for Brisbane and interstate markets.

ABOVE Rainforest and its wildlife are preserved in Lamington National Park on the south-eastern border between New South Wales and Queensland. Where the Elabana Falls spill from Canungra Creek, there is a stand of thousand-year-old Antarctic beech trees.

OPPOSITE In the Gold Coast hinterland are myriad rock pools, and one of the best known is Natural Arch, a summertime attraction for day-trippers retreating from the coast's humidity.

ABOVE Reminders of Brisbane's convict past on St Helena Island in Waterloo Bay. This was Queensland's high security jail from 1867 to 1932. It has also served as a quarantine station, and is now a national park.

Prison labour was used to construct all the early buildings from natural beach rock and island-made bricks. Accommodation was cramped. Cells of about 1.5m by 3m were shared by up to six prisoners who slept in two tiers of hammocks. From 1867 to 1890, prisoners were sent to St Helena for relatively minor offences but, from 1890 until 1921, it held murderers, rapists and other serious offenders. Legend has it that only one man made a successful escape from St Helena — in an accomplice's boat. Neglected for years, the island was taken over by the State Government in 1984 which undertook restoration and responsibility for preservation of the crumbling ruins.

The island, Waterloo Bay and the nearby mainland suburb of Wellington Point were named in the early days of settlement when Napoleon's defeat and place of exile were part of recent history.

OPPOSITE Graves as far as the eye can see. Toowong cemetery was founded in the 1870s and headstones from earlier cemeteries were moved there. The tall white column marks the grave of Governor Samuel Wensley Blackall who died on 2 January 1871. Among the headstones are those of Andrew Petrie, Moreton Bay's first free settler; his son John, the first Mayor of Brisbane after it was declared a municipality in 1859; Sir Samuel Griffith, a founding father of Australian Federation, the chief drafter of its constitution and first Chief Justice of the High Court; and the humourist Steele Rudd — whose real name was Arthur Hoey Davis.

Toowong was closed as a public cemetery in the 1960s but family plot burials still occur there and, with grave numbers of more than 150,000, it is one of the largest cemeteries in Australia.

BELOW This young John Bull is waving his Union Jack at a celebration commemorating the bicentenary of Matthew Flinders' landing on Coochie Mudlo Island in 1789.

These days Queenslanders, and Australians in general, acknowledge their situation as part of the Asia–Pacific region but traditional ties with the United Kingdom remain strong.

OPPOSITE The colourful red and black uniforms are those of the nineteenth century B Company, 1st Moreton Regiment, founded in 1886 and based at Fort Lytton at the mouth of the Brisbane River. Members of the Arms Collectors Guild don ceremonial dress on special occasions such as this colonial festival in the George Street Government Precinct.

OVERLEAF Not all the state's gracious homes are in Brisbane. Ipswich boasts buildings as beautiful as this one, *Belmont,* built in 1863 for Josiah Francis, a merchant from Adelaide, who became Mayor of Ipswich and a member of the Queensland Parliament (1881–1883). *Belmont,* built of rough-hewn stone — the front wall is half a metre thick — overlooks the playing fields of Ipswich Grammar School.

Relief sculptures and grotesques are carved into the
sandstone walls surrounding the Great Court of the
University of Queensland, the oldest and largest tertiary
institution in the state. Although the university did not
move to the St Lucia site until the 1950s, the sculptures
were begun in 1939 by Dresden–born John Muller. The
grotesques represent prominent scholars and academic
figures. This one is the work of Rhyl Hinwood who
became University Sculptor in 1976. It commemorates
Associate Professor Stanley Castlehow, member of the
Classics Department in the 1920s.

The University now has almost 20,000 students, and
sixty departments including the only mining engineering
school in an Australian university.

PREVIOUS PAGE Could there be a future world champion
— a Hayley Lewis or Tracey Wickham — in this primary
school swimming class at suburban Eagle Junction?
Swimming lessons are part of the curriculum for schools
throughout Queensland and provide a welcome break from
the classroom.

ABOVE Playtime at Eagle Junction Primary School.

OPPOSITE Proud of her violin, this primary school pupil
waits for a music lesson.

ABOVE Fun on wheels. These Brisbane youngsters enjoy one of the city's annual celebrations, the Australia Day picnic. Australia Day, 26 January, marks the anniversary of Captain Phillip's landing at Sydney Cove in 1788 and the beginning of European settlement in Australia — about 40,000 years after the arrival of the first Aborigines.

OPPOSITE Two young Aborigines prepare for a dance performance. The names given by their forebears are still borne by many Brisbane suburbs such as Enoggera (corroboree ground), Mount Coot-tha (mountain of honey) and Woolloongabba (place of the wallaby).

ABOVE Festivals encourage people to let their hair down, or should that be 'beard'? This character is enjoying the annual fair in Spring Hill, one of Brisbane's oldest suburbs — held in spring, of course. Streets are closed to traffic for stallholders to take over, and the festivities spread into neighbouring parks.

OPPOSITE Since 1962, September in Brisbane has meant the Warana Festival, two weeks of outdoor activities featuring a mix of free and ticket-only attractions. One of the most popular has been the Warana Parade which draws enormous crowds. Associated attractions include a Warana Writers' Week; art displays, an air pageant, jazz concerts, old-time dancing, cabarets and outdoor art exhibitions in the old Botanical Gardens.

ABOVE A discerning critic contemplates a work by Mark
Webb — *Abstract Painting (Before and After Science)* 1989 —
at the Queensland Art Gallery, part of the Cultural Centre
complex.

ABOVE The Queensland Ballet Company in a performance
of *Romeo and Juliet* at the Suncorp Theatre.

ABOVE Industrial sunset at Fisherman Island coal
terminal.

OPPOSITE An abseiler practises on the striking cliffs of
Kangaroo Point opposite Brisbane's city centre. These
cliffs, which provided stone for the retaining walls built
along the riverbank by convicts, are floodlit at night and a
great attraction for abseilers.

OVERLEAF The Great Dividing Range bathed in sunset's
eerie light.

PREVIOUS PAGE Mount Coot-tha seen from the city at sunset. The lookout at the top has long been a favourite beauty spot and early evening refuge from the heat of the city.

Chinese people first came to Queensland in search of gold soon after 1869 when it was found at Gympie, and some stayed on.

A Chinatown district has recently been established by the City Council as a cultural centre and tourist attraction. Chinese, Korean, Japanese, Singaporean and Thai restaurants make the district a gourmet's delight with specialty shops an added attraction.

ABOVE It would not be a Chinese festival without a noisy lion dance.

OPPOSITE Chinese citizens don traditional dress for the September Moon Festival celebrated in the Chinatown Mall.

ABOVE Two young dancers dressed for some strenuous
activity encourage passers-by to call in at a city nightclub.

OPPOSITE Headlights of evening peak-hour traffic make a
dazzling show on the Story Bridge which links the north
bank of the Brisbane River at Fortitude Valley to Kangaroo
Point on the south.

City Kaleidoscope

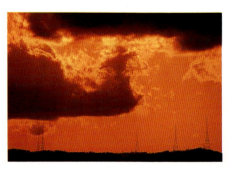